"A 'must read'—a tract for the times to call Christians to be Bible-based, Christ-centered, atonement-believing and -understanding, God-adoring people. Here is vintage J. I. Packer accompanied by some younger friends. The magisterial but too-little-known essay, 'What Did the Cross Achieve?' is itself worth the price of the whole book. And there is much more besides. Here, then, are gospel riches, and *In My Place Condemned He Stood* marks the spot where the buried treasure lies. Start digging!"

—Sinclair B. Ferguson, Senior Pastor, First Presbyterian Church, Columbia, South Carolina

"The essays in this volume by J. I. Packer are some of the most important things I have ever read. I'm delighted to see them united in one volume and supplemented by other excellent chapters and studies on this crucial topic. If you want to preach in such a way that results in real conversions and changed lives, you should master the approach to the cross laid out in this book."

—Tim Keller, Senior Pastor, Redeemer Presbyterian Church, New York City

"This book contains some of the finest essays that have ever been written on the death of Christ."

—David F. Wells, Andrew Mutch Distinguished Professor of Historical and Systematic Theology, Gordon-Conwell Theological Seminary

"What a joy and encouragement to have the three classic essays on the cross of Christ by J. I. Packer published in one volume. Furthermore, Mark Dever pierces to the marrow of the matter in his wonderfully clear essay on penal substitution. This book unpacks the significance of the cross so that we understand why we should glory only in the cross. Every student and pastor should own this volume, for the contents are so precious that they deserve more than one reading."

—Thomas R. Schreiner, James Buchanan Harrison Professor of New Testament Interpretation, The Southern Baptist Theological Seminary

"At a time when many are again questioning biblical fundamentals regarding atonement, secured for us by the death and resurrection of Christ, it is wonderful to see reprinted these four essays—each of which has proven to be enormously edifying to those who first read

them. Putting them together in this way was a brilliant idea. I heartily recommend the widespread distribution of this little book."

—D. A. Carson, Research Professor of New Testament,
Trinity Evangelical Divinity School

"In a time of spiritual decline and doctrinal confusion, it is desperately important for us to be clear about the cross. Writing with the precision of learned theologians and the passion of forgiven sinners, Mark Dever and J. I. Packer explain the meaning of atonement, substitution, and propitiation—not just as words, but as saving benefits we can only receive from a crucified Savior."

—Philip Graham Ryken, Senior Minister,
Tenth Presbyterian Church, Philadelphia

"It is common knowledge that J. I. Packer's introduction to John Owen's *The Death of Death in the Death of Christ* is worth the price of the book itself. But what a boon to have that same masterpiece bound in a single volume with his classic essays 'What Did the Cross Achieve?' and 'The Heart of the Gospel'—forming a theological treasure trove on the doctrine of penal substitutionary atonement. The addition to this magnificent theological triptych of Mark Dever's winsome and penetrating 'Nothing but the Blood' constitutes a mighty call to a Christ-centered, cruciform life. This is a book for our time—a galvanizing bulwark against today's attack upon the gospel of the cross of Christ."

—R. Kent Hughes, Senior Pastor Emeritus,
College Church, Wheaton, Illinois

"This edition is a splendid expression of the biblical doctrine of the atonement. Those who deny a personal penal substitution cannot account for the immense suffering of Christ or for the justification of the redeemed."

—Roger Nicole, Professor of Theology Emeritus,
Reformed Theological Seminary

"Given the current rebellion in many evangelical quarters against the biblical understanding of atonement, it is a great pleasure to see these classic essays of J. I. Packer once more in print, along with a new article by Mark Dever and a robust commendation by the four men behind Together for the Gospel. All those tired of the childish and therapeutic babble that passes for evangelical thought on the atonement these days will find this book to be an oasis in a dry and barren land."

—Carl R. Trueman, Academic Dean
and Professor of Historical Theology and Church History,
Westminster Theological Seminary, Philadelphia

"J. I. Packer and Mark Dever have done a superb job in pulling together into one volume some of the most critical doctrinal issues facing the church today. No one in the West or in developing countries who wants to preach or teach the heart of the gospel should miss reading, and rereading, these courageous articles on Christ's atonement for our sins. My prayer is that many copies of this book will come into the hands of those who preach and teach in Africa where doctrinally enlightening material such as this is scarce. It could go far in strengthening the church in Africa as it becomes the epicenter of Christianity."

—Rosemary Jensen, Founder and President, Rafiki Foundation

"This book joyfully exalts the doctrine of penal substitution in a biblical and orthodox theology. It is a wonderful gift to the church of the Lord Jesus, a church purchased by God with his own blood. Each of the contributors understands the crucial and essential necessity of grasping correctly the atoning work of Christ. He died in our place and paid in full the penalty of our sin. This book gets that right and I pray it will be widely read and carefully considered by all who love the Savior."

—Daniel L. Akin, President,
Southeastern Baptist Theological Seminary

"The first 'great' book I ever read was J. I. Packer's *Knowing God*. For fifty years he has showered the body of Christ with sound doctrine that clarifies and convicts. As believers in Christ, we can differ on many things but not the core message of the gospel itself. Once again J. I. Packer leads the way by producing with other capable scholars a clarification of the biblical gospel, our greatest treasure."

—James MacDonald, Pastor,
Harvest Bible Chapel, Rolling Meadows, Illinois

IN MY PLACE CONDEMNED HE STOOD

Celebrating the Glory of the Atonement

J. I. PACKER & MARK DEVER

Foreword by Ligon Duncan, R. Albert Mohler Jr.,
Mark Dever, and C. J. Mahaney

With an Annotated Bibliography
by Ligon Duncan

CROSSWAY BOOKS

WHEATON, ILLINOIS

Chapter 1, "The Heart of the Gospel": Chapter 18 of J. I. Packer's *Knowing God* (1973). Used by permission of Hodder & Stoughton Limited (Hatchette Livre UK Limited) and InterVarsity.

Chapter 2, "What Did the Cross Achieve?": J. I. Packer's Tyndale Biblical Theology Lecture, "What Did the Cross Achieve? The Logic of Penal Substitution" (1973). Used by permission of Tyndale House, Cambridge.

Chapter 3, "Nothing but the Blood": Mark Dever's article of the same title first appeared in *Christianity Today* (May 2006): 28-33.

Chapter 4, "Saved by His Precious Blood": J. I. Packer's introductory essay to John Owen's *The Death of Death in the Death of Christ* (1959). Used by permission of Banner of Truth Trust.

Cover design: Cindy Kiple
First printing 2008
Printed in the United States of America

Scripture quotations marked ESV are from *The Holy Bible, English Standard Version®*, copyright © 2001 by Crossway Bibles, a publishing ministry of Good News Publishers. Used by permission. All rights reserved.

Scripture references marked NIV are from *The Holy Bible: New International Version®*. Copyright © 1973, 1978, 1984 by International Bible Society. Used by permission of Zondervan Publishing House. All rights reserved.

The "NIV" and "New International Version" trademarks are registered in the United States Patent and Trademark Office by International Bible Society. Use of either trademark requires the permission of International Bible Society.

Scripture quotations marked KJV are from the *King James Version* of the Bible.

Scripture quotations marked RV are from the *Revised Version* of the Bible.

Scripture references marked NEB are from *The New English Bible®*. Copyright by the Delegates of the Oxford University Press and The Syndics of the Cambridge University Press, 1961, 1970.

Scripture references marked PHILLIPS are from *The New Testament in Modern English*, translated by J. B. Phillips © 1972 by J. B. Phillips. Published by Macmillan.

Scripture references marked RSV are from *The Revised Standard Version*. Copyright © 1946, 1952, 1971, 1973 by the Division of Christian Education of the National Council of the Churches of Christ in the U.S.A.

All emphases in Scripture quotations have been added by the author.

Library of Congress Cataloging-in-Publication Data

Packer, J. I. (James Innell).
    In my place condemned he stood : celebrating the glory of the atonement / J. I. Packer and Mark Dever.
        p. cm.
    Includes bibliographical references and index.
    ISBN 978-1-4335-0200-2 (tpb)
    1. Atonement. 2. Jesus Christ—Crucifixion. I. Dever, Mark. II. Title.
    BT265.3.P33 2008
    232'.3—dc22
                                    2007044611

BP	16	15	14	13	12	11	10	09	08
	9	8	7	6	5	4	3	2	1

To John Stott,
a faithful witness to the glory of the atonement.

Contents

Authors and Contributors   11

Foreword   13
  Ligon Duncan, R. Albert Mohler Jr., Mark Dever, and C. J. Mahaney

Preface: A Tract for the Times   17
  J. I. Packer and Mark Dever
Introduction: Penal Substitution Revisited   21
  J. I. Packer

1. The Heart of the Gospel   29
  J. I. Packer
2. What Did the Cross Achieve? The Logic of Penal Substitution   53
  J. I. Packer
3. Nothing but the Blood   101
  Mark Dever
4. Saved by His Precious Blood: An Introduction to John Owen's *The Death of Death in the Death of Christ*   111
  J. I. Packer

Epilogue: Christ-Centered Means
Cross-Centered   145
  J. I. Packer and Mark Dever
Books on the Cross of Christ   153
  Ligon Duncan
Annotated Bibliography   163
  Ligon Duncan

Authors and Contributors

J. I. Packer currently serves as a professor of theology at Regent College in Vancouver, British Columbia. Dr. Packer has written numerous books, including *Knowing God*. He served as general editor for the English Standard Version Bible, published by Crossway.

Mark Dever is senior pastor of Capitol Hill Baptist Church, Washington, DC, and executive director of 9Marks (www.9marks.org), a ministry for pastors and local churches.

Ligon Duncan is the senior minister of the historic First Presbyterian Church of Jackson, Mississippi, president of the Alliance of Confessing Evangelicals, and chairman of the Council on Biblical Manhood and Womanhood.

R. Albert Mohler Jr. serves as president of The Southern Baptist Theological Seminary in Louisville, Kentucky. Additionally, Dr. Mohler hosts a daily, live, nationwide radio program on the Salem Radio Network.

C. J. Mahaney leads Sovereign Grace Ministries, having pastored Covenant Life Church in Gaithersburg, Maryland, for twenty-seven years.

11

Man of Sorrows! what a name
For the Son of God, who came
Ruined sinners to reclaim:
Hallelujah, What a Savior!

Bearing shame and scoffing rude,
In my place condemned he stood;
Sealed my pardon with his blood:
Hallelujah! What a Savior!

Guilty, vile, and helpless, we;
Spotless Lamb of God was he.
Full atonement! Can it be?
Hallelujah! What a Savior!

Lifted up was he to die,
"It is finished!" was his cry;
Now in heaven, exalted high:
Hallelujah! What a Savior!

When he comes, our glorious King,
All his ransomed home to bring,
Then anew this song we'll sing:
Hallelujah! What a Savior!

—P. P. Bliss, 1838–1876

Foreword

The cross of Christ is at the very center of gospel proclamation, and thus a thorough, biblical grasp of this central truth is necessary for every gospel minister. Yet our day has seen (like ages before us) much confusion on this vital point of truth. This little book, *In My Place Condemned He Stood*, is offered as an aid and encouragement to Christians who want more deeply to understand the nature and accomplishments of Jesus' death and thus to be lost in wonder, love, and praise to the gracious Father who gave and delivered up his only begotten Son on our behalf, and to the Son who loved us and gave himself for us, by the Holy Spirit, who alone enables us to say truly, "Jesus is Lord."

The book that you are holding has a history. It exists, at least in part, because of the same friendships that brought us "Together for the Gospel." It contains what have already been reckoned classic, contemporary, evangelical essays on the subject of the atoning work of Christ. Al, Mark, C. J., and I (Ligon) were talking late one night (as is typical for us), and remarking on how singularly useful is J. I. Packer's introduction to John Owen's *The Death of Death in the Death of Christ* for articulating a robust, biblical view of salvation and for setting forth succinctly the Bible's teaching on the intent of the atoning work of Christ.

After a suitable season of reflection on our own first encounter with that piece, and how often it had been used to clarify the minds of growing Christians on the comforting truth of God's sovereignty in the salvation of sinners, we began to muse other choice, short pieces on the subject of the meaning and achievement of Christ's death on the cross. Almost simultaneously we named another famous Packer essay, "The Logic of Penal Substitution," given at Tyndale House many years ago. This essay is a little more academic than the Owen introduction, we all agreed, but it is solid gold, superb argument, sound, and edifying. Then one of us said, "Don't forget 'The Heart of the Gospel' from *Knowing God*"—yet another Packer piece that had pierced our hearts and grown us in grace.

I think it was Mark who then blurted aloud a thought, an idea, a wish: "Wouldn't it be great if all three of these were in one little book that you could give out to people who want to learn more about the atonement?" It was a stroke of genius, for all three of these short works are enormously helpful, devotionally powerful, and biblically faithful. We all hummed and nodded our agreement. "Yes, yes." But how would this happen?

It was agreed that Mark would call his old friend and senior colleague Jim Packer and inquire into his interest and willingness about such a project. Mark did. Dr. Packer graciously and enthusiastically consented, as did the good folks at Crossway. But Dr. Packer also suggested that Mark Dever's brilliant piece from *Christianity Today* be included. Mark protested mightily. "It doesn't remotely compare with the three works of yours, Jim." But Professor Packer was having nothing of it. "I insist," he said.

Then Mark asked me to do a brief annotated bibliography. "Please don't throw me in the briar patch," I thought to myself. What a joy to offer suggestions for further study on the work whereby our Savior ransomed, redeemed, and reconciled us, propitiating God's wrath by the Father's own loving design and expiating our sin by his blood and righteousness, by his whole, perfect obedience and penal substitutionary sacrifice. Well, it may not pass the test as brief, but I pray that it is useful nevertheless.

So that's how the book and the concept came together. Now it's up to you to read and be edified.

—Ligon Duncan

Ligon tells the story well. The book you now hold in your hands was born out of our shared concern that the eclipse and denial of this doctrine is endangering the health of the church. In these essays you will find a passionate and eloquent defense and exposition of the Bible's teaching that Christ "died for our sins, in accordance with the Scriptures" (1 Cor. 15:3). We believe this doctrine to be central and essential to the gospel. While the atonement accomplished by Christ cannot be reduced to this understanding alone (and no one should claim that it should), to deny or confuse this doctrine is to deny that Christ died on the cross *for our sins* and *as our substitute*. In other words, we honestly believe that those who deny, dismiss, and disparage this doctrine do injury to the gospel. If we truly stand together for the gospel, we stand together for the fact that Christ died on the cross as our substitute, paying the infinite penalty for our sins we could never pay. So read these essays, not only for the health of your soul, but for the health of the church.

—R. Albert Mohler Jr.

I have a couple of things to add. First, I believe this whole idea grew out of Al's certainty that we should address this issue—with which we all agreed. May God use our poor efforts (and Jim Packer's better ones) to aid his church in this. Second, Lig is correct in saying that I was reluctant to add my chapter to this volume. Anything I've said of enduring theological value on this topic is echoing Jim Packer, especially his lecture "What Did the Cross Achieve? The Logic of Penal Substitution." Many critics have suggested that proponents of penal substitution are trashing all other views, or at least ignoring them. I'm not sure I've ever read a book on the atonement that does this. Such a suggestion is, I think, theological caricature. The truth is that there is a soundly biblical and logically compelling case for considering various biblical images of the atonement, and the image of penal substitution is legitimately considered central. That is a more subtle argument, and Jim Packer makes it superbly. Okay, a third thing: don't miss Lig's bibliography at the end. Bibliographies are valuable—annotated bibliographies ten times more so. Lig has read for all of us, and he makes his reading available to us through his concise comments and summaries. Use and enjoy this little volume and be edified.

—Mark Dever

There is no true pastoral ministry apart from the cross. The cross must be central to all preaching and pastoring. In a day when the message of the cross is so often marginalized and its meaning so often undermined, these classic essays could hardly be more timely and relevant. They will help you love the Savior and serve the church he died for. So that's enough by us. Proceed immediately to the profound content of this little volume.

—C. J. Mahaney

Preface

A Tract for the Times

A century ago, G. K. Chesterton declared that it was beyond the wit of man to invent a new heresy. It seems that he was right, and that this is a truth to take to heart today. Heresies clothe themselves in up-to-date cultural garb and present themselves, face-lifted and iPod-armed, as the latest and wisest thing going, but current heresies, of which there are many, regularly prove, as their predecessors did, to be new forms of old mistakes. This book addresses what we see as a case in point.

We shall not, however, be calling it heresy, for this term today combines maximum fuzziness of meaning with maximum vituperative emotional heat. Such a word is literally too hot to handle in what purports to be sober analysis. We shall speak instead of unorthodoxy, a word that seems to us both more exact and less explosive.

Orthodoxy means right doctrinal belief, viewed as the church's confession of its faith and stated syllabus for teaching. Unorthodoxy means any deviation from that standard. It is, then, a form of unorthodoxy that we are currently seeking to counter.

Can we say that the Christian church, taken as a whole, actually has an orthodoxy? Some would say no, but our answer is yes. It is found in the churches' creeds and confessions, in their hymns and worship forms, and in the writings of their approved theologians. Does this orthodoxy extend to all the beliefs of all the churches? No. For example: on the nature and authority of the church and its clergy, on the number and working of the sacraments, and on the functioning of holy Scripture as a rule of faith and life, what is held as orthodox by Roman Catholicism and with less precision by Eastern Orthodoxy seems less than orthodox—unorthodox, therefore, or heterodox—to adherents of historic Protestant evangelicalism; and Protestantism itself is split down the middle on some secondary matters, such as whether baptizing believers' infants is part of God's prescribed way or not. The present writers, an elderly Canadian Anglican and a middle-aged Southern Baptist, heartily disagree on that subject, though on everything of prime importance, as we see it, such as the truth of the Trinity and of the incarnation, all humanity's need for salvation from the guilt and power of sin, the present heavenly reign and future visible return of the Lord Jesus Christ, and the way of salvation through faith, and faith alone, in him, we regard each other as a standard and bastion of orthodoxy. What we now seek to meet is a challenge to the truly catholic and truly evangelical belief system that we share.

No recognized name exists for the unorthodoxy that we have in view, so we coin one. On the model of anti-Trinitarianism, a fairly familiar term with a clear meaning, and anti-incarnationalism, a word less common but no less clear, we label the generic error we are up against *anti-redemptionism*. Its essence is sidelining, and in some cases actually denying, the work of Jesus Christ as our redeemer, who did all that had to be done to save us from hell, in favor of the idea of Jesus as teacher, model, and pioneer of godliness. Methodologically, in having Christ's prophetic word thus trump his priestly work, ancient Graeco-Roman Gnosticism and modern Western Protestant liberalism join hands (in a high-five, one might almost say), though, since the preexisting cultural frames into which Jesus' teaching is then made to fit are very different, the results of following the method vary very much also. But the substantive unorthodoxy of this nonbiblical method of proceeding is common to them both.

A recent twist in Western liberal unorthodoxy is to say that all accounts of the redemptive work of Christ on the cross must be judged immoral, since violence as such is always immoral, and since penal substitution explicitly ascribes the violence that Jesus suffered to the Father, penal substitution is the most immoral account of all. In this fashion, fueled by one culturally projected, anti-redemptionist axiom after another, the critique of orthodoxy goes on.

It has been said that the best defense of any doctrine is the creative exposition of it. That is the star by which we steer; that is what we hope we have achieved in this book. Apart from the present preface and the epilogue, which are joint efforts, all the pieces that follow are compositions by one or other of us that have received a measure of approval and which, we think, make together a cumulative expository case. J. I. Packer's "Penal Substitution Revisited" was published in a slightly shorter form in *NB: News*, British UCCF's house magazine, July 2007. "The Heart of the Gospel" is chapter 18 of his *Knowing God* (1973). "What Did the Cross Achieve? The Logic of Penal Substitution" first appeared in *Tyndale Bulletin* 25 (1974; pp. 3–45). "Saved by His Precious Blood" was written to introduce a reprint of John Owen, *The Death of Death in the Death of Christ* (1648) in 1958, and is now chapter 8 of *A Quest for Godliness* (in Britain, *Among God's Giants*, 1990). Mark Dever's "Nothing but the Blood" was published in *Christianity Today*, May 2006.

We offer this book not as a treatise but as a testimony and a composite tract for the times. Our prayer is that God will use it to help his children distinguish things that differ, and to ground them more thoroughly in the truth of Christ.

J. I. Packer
Mark Dever

Introduction

Penal Substitution Revisited

J. I. Packer

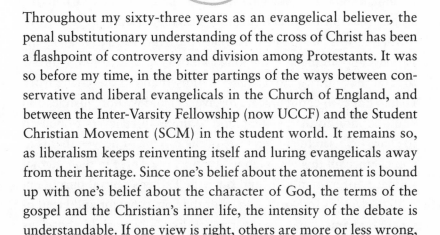

Throughout my sixty-three years as an evangelical believer, the penal substitutionary understanding of the cross of Christ has been a flashpoint of controversy and division among Protestants. It was so before my time, in the bitter partings of the ways between conservative and liberal evangelicals in the Church of England, and between the Inter-Varsity Fellowship (now UCCF) and the Student Christian Movement (SCM) in the student world. It remains so, as liberalism keeps reinventing itself and luring evangelicals away from their heritage. Since one's belief about the atonement is bound up with one's belief about the character of God, the terms of the gospel and the Christian's inner life, the intensity of the debate is understandable. If one view is right, others are more or less wrong, and the definition of Christianity itself comes to be at stake.

An evangelical theologian, dying, cabled a colleague: "I am so thankful for the active obedience [righteousness] of Christ. No hope without it." As I grow old I want to tell everyone who will listen: "I am so thankful for the penal substitutionary death of Christ. No hope without it." That is where I come from now as I attempt this brief vindication of the best part of the best news that the world has ever heard.

The Atonement in Focus

It is impossible to focus the atonement properly until the biblical mode of Trinitarian and incarnational thought about Jesus Christ is embraced. The Trinitarian principle is that the three distinct persons within the divine unity—the Father, the Son, and the Holy Spirit—always work inseparably together, as in creation, so in providence and in every aspect of the work of redemption. The incarnational principle is that when the Son took to himself all the powers and capacities for experience that belong to human nature and began to live through his human body, mind, and identity, his sense of being the Father's Son was unaffected, and he knew and did his Father's will, aided by the Spirit, at all times. It was with his own will and his own love mirroring the Father's, therefore, that he took the place of human sinners exposed to divine judgment and laid down his life as a sacrifice for them, entering fully into the state and experience of death that was due to them. Then he rose from death to reign by the Father's appointment in the kingdom of God and from his throne to send the Spirit to induce faith in himself and in the saving work he had done, to communicate forgiveness and pardon, justification and adoption to the penitent, and to unite all believers to himself to share his risen life in foretaste of the full life of heaven that is to come. Since all this was planned by the holy Three in their eternal solidarity of mutual love, and since the Father's central purpose in it all was and is to glorify and exalt the Son as Savior and Head of a new humanity, smartypants notions like "divine child abuse" as a comment on the cross are supremely silly and as irreverent and wrong as they could possibly be.

As in all the Creator's interacting with the created order, there is here an element of transcendent mystery, comparable to fog in the distance hanging around a landscape that the rising sun has effectively cleared for our view. What is stated above is clearly revealed in God's own witness to himself in the Bible, and so must be given the status of nonnegotiable fact.

Again, the atonement cannot be focused properly where the biblical view of God's justice as one facet of his holiness and of human willfulness as the root of our racial, communal, and personal sinfulness and guilt, is not grasped. Justice as such, as Aristotle said long ago, is essentially giving everyone their due, and whatever more God's justice (righteousness) means in the Bible it certainly starts here, with retribution for wrongdoing. We see this as early as Genesis 3 and as late as Revelation 22:18–19 and consistently in between. God's mercy to guilty sinners is framed by his holy hostility (wrath) against their sins.

For human nature is radically twisted into an instinctive yet deliberate and ineradicable habit of God-defying or God-denying self-service, so that God's requirement of perfect love to himself and others is permanently beyond our reach, and falling short of God's standard marks our lives every day. What is due to us, then, from God is condemnation and rejection.

Penal Substitution in Focus

The built-in function of the human mind that we call conscience tells everyone, uncomfortably, that when we have misbehaved we ought to suffer for it, and to that extent conscience is truly the voice of God.

Both Testaments, then, confirm that judicial retribution from God awaits all whose sins are not covered by a substitutionary sacrifice: in the Old Testament, the sacrifice of an animal; in the New Testament, the sacrifice of Christ. He, the holy Son of God in sinless human flesh, has endured what Calvin called "the pains of a condemned and lost person" so that we, trusting him as our Savior and Lord, might receive pardon for the past and a new life in him and with him for the present and the future. Tellingly Paul, having announced "the redemption that is in Christ Jesus, whom God put forward as a propitiation [i.e., wrath-quencher] by his blood, to be received by faith," goes on to say: "It was to show his righteousness at the present time, so that he might be *just and* the justifier of the one who has faith in Jesus" (Rom. 3:24–26 ESV). *Just* justification—*justified* justification—through the doing of justice in penal substitution is integral to the message of the gospel.

Penal substitution, therefore, will not be focused properly till it is recognized that God's redemptive love must not be conceived—misconceived, rather—as somehow trumping and displacing God's retributive justice, as if the Creator-Judge simply decided to let bygones be bygones. The measure of God's holy love for us is that "while we were still sinners, Christ died for us" and that "he . . . did not spare his own Son but gave him up for us all" (Rom. 5:8; 8:32 ESV). Evidently there was no alternative to paying that price if we were to be saved, so the Son at the Father's behest, "through the eternal Spirit" (Heb. 9:14), paid it. Thus God "set aside" "the record of debt that stood against us . . . nailing it to the cross" (Col. 2:14 ESV). Had we been among the watchers at Calvary, we should have seen nailed to the cross Pilate's notice of Jesus' alleged crime. But if by faith we look back to Calvary from where we now are, what we see is the list of our own unpaid debts of obedience to God, for which Christ paid the penalty in our place. Paul, having himself learned to do this, testified: "The life I now live in the flesh I live by faith in the Son of God, who loved me and gave himself for me" (Gal. 2:20 ESV).

It is often pointed out that Paul uses a wide variety of analogical images to express what Christ achieved for humanity on the cross. Yes, but these are not coordinates in a loosely textured matrix of endlessly exploratory thinking, as tends to be assumed; rather, in Paul's very clear and orderly mind, they form a logical and theological hierarchy, thus:

How did Christ's sacrificial death actually save us—that is, rescue us from jeopardy and ruin? By *redeeming* us, which means effecting our transfer from a state of bondage without hope to a state of freedom with a future, by paying the price that the transfer required. Thus slaves were bought out of servitude in Paul's day. The more remote background is God's redeeming Israel from

Egyptian captivity "by a mighty hand." (See Rom. 3:24; Gal. 3:13, 4:5; Eph. 1:7.)

The Essence of the Atonement

How then did the cross actually redeem us, through Jesus' death? By *reconciling* us to God, ending the alienation and estrangement that were previously there, linking God and us together in new harmony, replacing enmity between us with friendship and peace, by means of the putting away of our sins. (See Rom. 5:11; Col. 1:19–22.)

So how did the cross actually reconcile us to God, and God to us? By being a *propitiation*, ending God's judicial wrath against us. (See Rom. 3:24.)

And how did the cross actually propitiate God? By being an event of *substitution*, whereby at the Father's will the sinless Son bore the retribution due to us guilty ones. (See 2 Cor. 5:21; Gal. 3:13; Col. 2:14.)

For Paul, this substitution, Christ bearing our penalty in our place, is the essence of the atonement. Certainly, he celebrates the cross as a victory over the forces of evil on our behalf (Col. 2:15) and as a motivating revelation of the love of God toward us (2 Cor. 5:14–15), but if it had not been an event of penal substitution, it would not for him have been either of these. As Galatians 2:20 declares, his life of responsive faith was wholly formed and driven by the knowledge that his Savior had revealed divine love to him by giving himself to die on the cross in order to save him.

Accordingly, this text starts to show us how faith in Christ, our penal substitute, should be shaping our own lives today, which will be my final point for reflection. Thirty years ago I wrote an analysis of insights basic to personal religion that faith in Christ as one's penal substitute yields. Since I cannot today improve on it, I cite it as it stands.

1) God, in Denney's phrase, "condones nothing," but judges all sin as it deserves: which Scripture affirms, and my conscience confirms, to be right.

2) My sins merit ultimate penal suffering and rejection from God's presence (conscience also confirms this), and nothing I do can blot them out.

3) The penalty due to me for my sins, whatever it was, was paid for me by Jesus Christ, the Son of God, in his death on the cross.

4) Because this is so, I through faith in him am made "the righteousness of God in him," i.e., I am justified; pardon, acceptance, and sonship [to God] become mine.

5) Christ's death for me is my sole ground of hope before God. "If he fulfilled not justice, I must; if he underwent not wrath, I must to eternity" (John Owen).

6) My faith in Christ is God's own gift to me, given in virtue of Christ's death for me: i.e., the cross procured it.

7) Christ's death for me guarantees my preservation to glory.

8) Christ's death for me is the measure and pledge of the love of the Father and the Son to me.

9) Christ's death for me calls and constrains me to trust, to worship, to love, and to serve.[1]

Only where these nine truths have taken root and grow in the heart will anyone be fully alive to God.

A lawyer, having completed his argument, may declare that here he rests his case. I, having surveyed the penal substitutionary sacrifice of Christ afresh, now reaffirm that here I rest my hope. So, I believe, will all truly faithful believers.

In recent years, great strides in biblical theology and contemporary canonical exegesis have brought new precision to our grasp of the Bible's overall story of how God's plan to bless Israel, and through Israel the world, came to its climax in and through Christ. But I do not see how it can be denied that each New Testament book, whatever other job it may be doing, has in view, one way or another, Luther's primary question: how may a weak, perverse, and guilty sinner find a gracious God? Nor can it be denied that real

1. Cited from *Tyndale Bulletin* 25, 1974, 42–43.

Christianity only really starts when that discovery is made. And to the extent that modern developments, by filling our horizon with the great metanarrative, distract us from pursuing Luther's question in personal terms, they hinder as well as help in our appreciation of the gospel.

The church is and will always be at its healthiest when every Christian can line up with every other Christian to sing (or, in these musically dizzy days, to learn to sing) P. P. Bliss's simple words, which really say it all:

> Bearing shame and scoffing rude
> In my place condemned he stood,
> Sealed my pardon with his blood—
> Hallelujah! What a Saviour!

1

The Heart of the Gospel

J. I. Packer

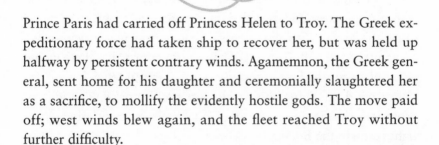

Prince Paris had carried off Princess Helen to Troy. The Greek expeditionary force had taken ship to recover her, but was held up halfway by persistent contrary winds. Agamemnon, the Greek general, sent home for his daughter and ceremonially slaughtered her as a sacrifice, to mollify the evidently hostile gods. The move paid off; west winds blew again, and the fleet reached Troy without further difficulty.

This bit of the Trojan War legend, which dates from about 1000 B.C., mirrors an idea of propitiation on which pagan religion all over the world, and in every age, has been built. The idea is as follows. There are various gods, none enjoying absolute dominion, but each with some power to make life easier or harder for you. Their temper is uniformly uncertain; they take offense at the smallest things—or they get jealous because they feel you are paying too much attention to other gods and other people and not enough to themselves, and then they take it out on you by manipulating circumstances to your hurt.

Pagan Propitiation

The only course at that point is to humor and mollify them by an offering. The rule with offerings is the bigger the better, for the gods are inclined to hold out for something sizeable. In this they are cruel and heartless, but they have the advantage, so what can you do? The wise person bows to the inevitable and makes sure to offer something impressive enough to produce the desired result. Human sacrifice, in particular, is expensive but effective. Thus pagan religion appears as a callous commercialism, a matter of managing and manipulating your gods by cunning bribery. And within paganism propitiation, the appeasing of celestial bad tempers takes its place as a regular part of life, one of the many irksome necessities that one cannot get on without.

Now, the Bible takes us right away from the world of pagan religion. It condemns paganism out of hand as a monstrous distortion of truth. In place of a cluster of gods who are all too obviously made in the image of man, and who behave like a crowd of Hollywood film stars, the Bible sets the one almighty Creator, the only real God, in whom all goodness and truth find their source, and to whom all moral evil is abhorrent. With him there is no bad temper, no capriciousness, no vanity, no ill will. One might expect, therefore, that there would be no place for the idea of propitiation in biblical religion.

But we do not find this at all: just the opposite. The idea of propitiation—that is, of averting God's anger by an offering—runs right through the Bible.

Propitiation in the Bible

In the Old Testament, it underlies the prescribed rituals of the sin offering, the guilt offering ("trespass-offering" in the KJV), and the day of atonement (Lev. 4:1–6:7; 16:1–34); also, it finds clear expression in such narratives as that of Numbers 16:41–50, where God threatens to destroy the people for maligning his judgment on Korah, Dathan, and Abiram: "Then Moses said to Aaron, 'Take your censer and put incense in it, along with fire from the altar, and hurry to the assembly to make atonement for them. Wrath has come out from the LORD; the plague has started.' . . . So Aaron . . . made atonement for them. . . . And the plague stopped" (vv. 46–48).[1]

In the New Testament, the *propitiation* word group appears in four passages of such transcendent importance that we may well pause to set them out in full.

The first is Paul's classic statement of *the rationale of God's justification of sinners.*

"But now apart from the law a righteousness of God hath been manifested . . . even the righteousness of God through faith in Jesus Christ unto all them that believe; for there is no distinction; for all have sinned, and fall short of the glory of God; being justified freely by his grace through the redemption that is in Christ Jesus: whom God set forth to be a *propitiation,* through faith, by his blood, to show his righteousness, because of the passing over of the sins done aforetime, in the forbearance of God; for the shewing, I say, of his righteousness at this present season: that he might himself be just, and the justifier of him that hath faith in Jesus" (Rom. 3:21–26 RV).

The second is part of the exposition in Hebrews of *the rationale of the incarnation of God the Son.*

"It behooved him in all things to be made like unto his brethren, that he might be a merciful and faithful high priest, in things pertaining to God, to make *propitiation* for the sins of the people" (Heb. 2:17 RV).

The third is John's testimony to *the heavenly ministry of our Lord.*

"If any man sin, we have an advocate with the Father, Jesus Christ the righteous: and he is the *propitiation* for our sins" (1 John 2:1–2 KJV).

The fourth is John's *definition of the love of God.*

"God is love. In this was manifested the love of God toward us, because that God sent his only begotten Son into the world, that we might live through him. Herein is love, not that we loved God, but that he loved us, and sent his Son to be the *propitiation* for our sins" (1 John 4:8–10).

---

1. Unless otherwise indicated, Scripture quotations in this chapter are from the New International Version (NIV).

Has the word *propitiation* any place in your Christianity? In the faith of the New Testament it is central. The love of God, the taking of human form by the Son, the meaning of the cross, Christ's heavenly intercession, the way of salvation—all are to be explained in terms of it, as the passages quoted show, and any explanation from which the thought of propitiation is missing will be incomplete, and indeed actually misleading, by New Testament standards.

In saying this, we swim against the stream of much modern teaching and condemn at a stroke the views of a great number of distinguished church leaders today, but we cannot help that. Paul wrote, "Even if we or an angel from heaven"—let alone a minister, bishop, college lecturer, university professor, or noted author—"should preach a gospel other than the one we preached to you, let him be eternally condemned!" ("accursed" KJV and RSV; "outcast" NEB; "damned" PHILLIPS— Gal. 1:8). And a gospel without propitiation at its heart is another gospel than that which Paul preached. The implications of this must not be evaded.

Not Merely Expiation

If, however, you look at the RSV or NEB versions of the four texts quoted above, you will find that the word *propitiation* does not appear. In both the 1 John passages, NEB has "remedy for the defilement" of our sins; elsewhere, these versions replace the thought of *propitiation* by that of *expiation*. What is the difference? The difference is that expiation means only half of what propitiation means. Expiation is an action that has sin as its object; it denotes the covering, putting away, or rubbing out of sin so that it no longer constitutes a barrier to friendly fellowship between man and God. Propitiation, however, in the Bible, denotes all that expiation means, *and the pacifying of the wrath of God thereby*. So, at any rate, Christian scholars have maintained since the Reformation, when these things first began to be studied with precision, and the case can still be made compellingly today.[2]

2. See Leon Morris, *The Apostolic Preaching of the Cross* (Grand Rapids, MI: Eerdmans, 1955), 125–85, for one example.

But in this century a number of scholars, notably C. H. Dodd, have revived the view of the sixteenth-century Unitarian Socinus, a view that had already been picked up in the late 1800s by Albrecht Ritschl, a founder of German liberalism, to the effect that there is in God no such thing as anger occasioned by human sin, and consequently no need or possibility of propitiation. Dodd has labored to prove that the *propitiation* word group in the New Testament does not carry the sense of appeasing God's anger but only denotes the putting away of sin, and that therefore *expiation* is a better rendering; and the RSV and NEB at this point reflect his view.

Does he make out his case? We cannot here go into the technicalities of what is very much a scholars' discussion; but, for what it is worth, we give our own verdict. Dodd, it appears, has shown that this word group *need* not mean more than expiation if the context does not require a wider meaning, but he has not shown that the word group *cannot* mean propitiation in contexts where this meaning is called for. This, however, is the crucial point: in the epistle to the Romans (to take the clearest and most obvious of the four passages) the context *does* call for the meaning *propitiation* in 3:25.

For in Romans 1:18 Paul sets the stage for his declaration of the gospel by affirming that "the wrath of God is revealed from heaven against all ungodliness and unrighteousness of men." "The wrath of God is dynamically, effectively operative in the world of men and it is as proceeding from heaven, the throne of God, that it is thus active."[3] In the rest of Romans 1 Paul traces out the present activity of God's wrath in the judicial hardening of apostate hearts, expressed in the thrice-repeated phrase "God gave them up" (vv. 24, 26, 28 KJV).

Then in Romans 2:1–16 Paul confronts us with the certainty of the "day of wrath and revelation of the righteous judgment of God; who will render to every man according to his works: . . . unto them that . . . obey not the truth, but obey unrighteousness, shall be wrath

3. John Murray, *The Epistle to the Romans* (Grand Rapids, MI: Eerdmans, 1997), 1:34.

and indignation . . . in the day when God shall judge the secrets of men, according to my gospel, by Jesus Christ" (vv. 5–6, 8, 16 RV).

In the first part of Romans 3, Paul carries on his argument to prove that every man, Jew and Gentile alike, being "under sin" (v. 9), stands exposed to the wrath of God in both its present and future manifestation. Here, then, are all of us in our natural state, without the gospel; the finally controlling reality in our lives, whether we are aware of it or not, is the active anger of God. But now, says Paul, acceptance, pardon, and peace, are freely given to those who hitherto were "wicked" (4:5) and "God's enemies" (5:10), but who now put faith in Christ Jesus, "whom God set forth to be a propitiation . . . by his blood." And believers know that "much more then, being now justified by his blood, shall we be saved from the wrath of God through him" (5:9 RV).

What has happened? The wrath of God against us, both present and to come, has been quenched. How was this effected? Through the death of Christ. "When we were enemies, we were reconciled to God through the death of his Son" (5:10). The "blood"—that is, the sacrificial death—of Jesus Christ abolished God's anger against us and ensured that his treatment of us forever after would be propitious and favorable. Henceforth, instead of showing himself to be against us, he would show himself in our life and experience to be for us. What, then, does the phrase "a propitiation . . . by his blood" express? It expresses, in the context of Paul's argument, precisely this thought: that *by his sacrificial death for our sins Christ pacified the wrath of God.*

It is true that a generation ago Dodd tried to evade this conclusion by arguing that the wrath of God in Romans is an impersonal cosmic principle of retribution in which the mind and heart of God toward men do not find true expression—that, in other words, God's wrath is a process external to the will of God himself. But it is now increasingly admitted that this attempt was a gallant failure. "It is inadequate," writes R. V. G. Tasker, "to regard this term [wrath] merely as a description of 'the inevitable process of cause and effect in a moral universe' or as another way of speaking of the results of sin.

It is rather a personal quality, without which God would cease to be fully righteous and his love would degenerate into sentimentality."[4] The wrath of God is as personal, and as potent, as his love; and, just as the blood-shedding of the Lord Jesus was the direct manifesting of his Father's love toward us, so it was the direct averting of his Father's wrath against us.

God's Anger

What manner of thing is the wrath of God that was propitiated at Calvary?

It is not the capricious, arbitrary, bad-tempered, and conceited anger that pagans attribute to their gods. It is not the sinful, resentful, malicious, infantile anger that we find among humans. It is a function of that holiness which is expressed in the demands of God's moral law ("be holy, because I am holy" [1 Pet. 1:16]), and of that righteousness which is expressed in God's acts of judgment and reward. "We know who it is that has said, 'Justice is mine: I will repay'" (Heb. 10:30 NEB).

God's wrath is "the holy revulsion of God's being against that which is the contradiction of his holiness"; it issues in "a positive outgoing of the divine displeasure."[5] And this is *righteous* anger—the *right* reaction of moral perfection in the Creator toward moral perversity in the creature. So far from the manifestation of God's wrath in punishing sin being morally doubtful, the thing that would be morally doubtful would be for him *not* to show his wrath in this way. God is not *just*—that is, he does not act in the way that is *right*, he does not do what is proper to a *judge*—unless he inflicts upon all sin and wrongdoing the penalty it deserves. We shall see Paul himself arguing on this basis in a moment.

Propitiation Described

Note, now, three facts about the propitiation, as Paul describes it.

---

4. *New Bible Dictionary*, s.v. "wrath."
5. John Murray, *Epistle to the Romans*.

1) *Propitiation is the work of God himself.* In paganism, man propitiates his gods, and religion becomes a form of commercialism and, indeed, of bribery. In Christianity, however, God propitiates his wrath by his own action. *He set forth Jesus Christ,* says Paul, to be a propitiation; *he sent his Son,* says John, to be the propitiation for our sins. It was not man, to whom God was hostile, who took the initiative to make God friendly, nor was it Jesus Christ, the eternal Son, who took the initiative to turn his Father's wrath against us into love. The idea that the kind Son changed the mind of his unkind Father by offering himself in place of sinful man is no part of the gospel message—it is a sub-Christian, indeed an anti-Christian, idea, for it denies the unity of will in the Father and the Son and so in reality falls back into polytheism, asking us to believe in two different gods. But the Bible rules this out absolutely by insisting that it was God himself who took the initiative in quenching his own wrath against those whom, despite their ill-desert, he loved and had chosen to save.

> The doctrine of the propitiation is precisely this: that God loved the objects of His wrath so much that He gave His own Son to the end that He by His blood should make provision for the removal of His wrath. It was Christ's so to deal with the wrath that the loved would no longer be the objects of wrath, and love would achieve its aim of making the children of wrath the children of God's good pleasure.[6]

Paul and John both state this explicitly and emphatically. God reveals his righteousness, says Paul, not only in retribution and judgment according to his law, but also "apart from the law," in bestowing righteousness on those who put faith in Jesus Christ. They have all sinned, yet they are all justified (acquitted, accepted, reinstated, set right with God) freely and for nothing (Rom. 3:21–24). How does this take place? "By grace" (that is, mercy contrary to merit; love for the unlovely and, one would have said, unlovable.) By what means does grace operate? "Through the redemption [rescue by ransom]

6. John Murray, *The Atonement* (Philadelphia: Presbyterian and Reformed, 1962), 15.

that is in Christ Jesus." How is it that, to those who put faith in him, Christ Jesus is the source, means, and substance of redemption? Because, says Paul, God set him forth to be a propitiation. From this divine initiative the reality and availability of redemption flow.

Love to one another, says John, is the family likeness of God's children; he who does not love Christians is evidently not in the family, for "God is love" and imparts a loving nature to all who know him (1 John 4:7–8). But "God is love" is a vague formula; how can we form a clear idea of the love that God would reproduce in us? "This is how God showed his love among us: he sent his one and only Son into the world that we might live through him" (1 John 4:9). Nor was this done as God's acknowledgement of some real devotion on our part; not at all. "Herein is love, not that we loved God but that"—in a situation where we did not love him, and there was nothing about us to move him to do anything other than blast and blight us for our ingrained irreligion—"he loved us, and sent his Son to be the propitiation for our sins." By this divine initiative, says John, the meaning and measure of the love that we must imitate are made known.

The witness of both apostles to God's initiative in propitiation could scarcely be clearer.

2) *Propitiation was made by the death of Jesus Christ. Blood*, as we hinted earlier, is a word pointing to the violent death inflicted in the animal sacrifices of the old covenant. God himself instituted these sacrifices by his own command, and in Leviticus 17:11 he says why: "For the life of a creature is in the blood, and I have given it to you to make atonement for yourselves on the altar; it is the blood that makes atonement." When Paul tells us that God set forth Jesus to be a propitiation "by his blood," his point is that what quenched God's wrath and so redeemed us from death was not Jesus' life or teaching, not his moral perfection nor his fidelity to the Father, as such, but the shedding of his blood in death. Along with the other New Testament writers, Paul always points to the death of Jesus as the atoning event and explains the atonement in terms of *representative substitution*—the innocent taking place of the guilty, in the

name and for the sake of the guilty, under the axe of God's judicial retribution. Two passages may be quoted to illustrate this.

"Christ redeemed us from the curse of the law"—how?—"by becoming a curse for us" (Gal. 3:13). Christ bore the curse of the law, which was directed against us, so that we might not have to bear it. This is representative substitution.

"One died for all," and through Jesus' death God was "reconciling the world unto himself." What does this reconciliation involve? "Not counting men's sins against them" but causing them in Christ to become "the righteousness of God"—that is, accepted as righteous by God. How is this nonimputation brought about? Through the imputing of our trespasses to another, who bore their due. "God made him who had no sin to be sin for us." It thus appears that it was as a sacrifice for sinners, enduring the death penalty in their stead, that "one died for all" (2 Cor. 5:14, 18–21). This is representative substitution.

Representative substitution, as the way and means of atonement, was taught in typical form by the God-given Old Testament sacrificial system. There, the perfect animal that was to be offered for sin was first symbolically constituted a *representative* by the sinner's laying his hand on its head and so identifying it with him and him with it (Lev. 4:4, 24, 29, 33), and then it was killed as a *substitute* for the offerer, the blood being sprinkled "before the Lord" and applied to one or both of the altars in the sanctuary (Lev. 4:6–7, 17–18, 25, 30) as a sign that expiation had been made, averting wrath and restoring fellowship.

On the annual Day of Atonement, two goats were used. One was killed as a sin offering in the ordinary way, and the other, after the priest had laid hands on its head and put Israel's sins "on the head" of the animal by confessing them there, was sent away to "bear upon him all their iniquities unto a land not inhabited" (Lev. 16:21–22). This double ritual taught a single lesson: that through the sacrifice of a representative substitute God's wrath is averted and that sins are borne away out of sight, never to trouble our relationship with God again. The second goat (the scapegoat) illustrates what, in terms of the type, was accomplished by the death of the first goat. These rituals are the immediate background of Paul's teaching on propitiation; it is the fulfillment of the Old Testament sacrificial pattern that he proclaims.

3) *Propitiation manifests God's righteousness.* So far from calling into question the morality of God's way of dealing with sin, says Paul, the truth of propitiation establishes it and was explicitly intended to establish it. God set forth his Son to propitiate his own wrath "to declare His *righteousness* [justice] . . . that He might be *just, and* the justifier of him which believeth in Jesus" (Rom. 3:25–26 KJV). The word "declare" implies a public display. Paul's point is that the public spectacle of propitiation, at the cross, was a public manifestation, not merely of justifying mercy on God's part, but of righteousness and justice as the basis of justifying mercy.

Such a manifestation was needed, says Paul, "because of the passing over of the sins done aforetime, in the forbearance of God." The point here is that though human beings were, and had been from time immemorial, every bit as bad as Romans 1 depicts them, God had not at any time since the flood made it his principle to deal publicly with the race as it deserved. Though people since the flood have been no better than their forebears were before the flood, God had not reacted to their impenitence and irreligion and lawlessness by public acts of adverse providence. Instead, he "has shown kindness by giving you rain from heaven and crops in their seasons; he provides you with plenty of food and fills your hearts with joy" (Acts 14:17).

This "passing over" of sins in "forbearance" was not, indeed, forgiveness, but postponement of judgment only; nevertheless, it prompts a question. If, as happens, humans do evil, and the Judge of all the earth continues to do them good, can he be as concerned about morality and godliness, the distinction between right and wrong in the lives of his creatures, as he formerly appeared to be, and as perfect justice would seem to require? Indeed, if he allows sinners to continue unpunished, does he not himself come short of perfection in his office as Judge of the world?

Paul has already answered the second part of this question by his doctrine of "the day of God's wrath" and "righteous judgment" in Romans 2:1–16. Here he answers the first part by saying in effect that God, far from being unconcerned about moral issues and the just requirement of retribution for wrongdoing, is so concerned about these things that he does not—indeed, Paul would, we think, boldly say, cannot—pardon sinners, and justify the ungodly, except on the basis of justice shown forth in retribution. Our sins *have been* punished; the wheel of retribution *has* turned; judgment *has* been inflicted for our ungodliness—but on Jesus, the lamb of God, standing in our place. In this way God is *just—and* the justifier of those who put faith in Jesus, "who was delivered over to death for our sins and was raised to life for our justification" (Rom. 4:25).

Thus the righteousness of God the Judge, which is set forth so vividly in the doctrine of divine wrath in the first part of Paul's letter, is set forth again in Paul's doctrine of how divine wrath was quenched. It is vital to his argument to show that the truths of salvation and damnation alike manifest the essential, inherent retributive justice that belongs to the divine character. In each case—the salvation of those who are saved, and the damnation of those who are lost—retribution falls; punishment is inflicted; God is righteous, and justice is done.

The Death of Christ

What we have said so far may be summed up as follows. The gospel tells us that our Creator has become our Redeemer. It announces that the Son of God has become man "for us men and for our salvation" and has died on the cross to save us from eternal judgment. The basic description of the saving death of Christ in the Bible is as a *propitiation,* that is, as that which quenched God's wrath against us by obliterating our sins from his sight. God's wrath is his righteousness reacting against unrighteousness; it shows itself in retributive justice. But Jesus Christ has shielded us from the nightmare prospect of retributive justice by becoming our representative substitute, in obedience to his Father's will, and receiving the wages of our sin in our place.

By this means justice has been done, for the sins of all that will ever be pardoned were judged and punished in the person of God the Son, and it is on this basis that pardon is now offered to us offenders. Redeeming love and retributive justice joined hands, so to speak, at Calvary, for there God showed himself to be "just, and the justifier of him that hath faith in Jesus."

Do you understand this? If you do, you are now seeing to the very heart of the Christian gospel. No version of that message goes deeper than that which declares man's root problem before God to be his sin, which evokes wrath, and God's basic provision for man to be propitiation, which out of wrath brings peace. Some versions of the gospel, indeed, are open to blame because they never get down to this level.

We have all heard the gospel presented as God's triumphant answer to human problems—problems of our relation with ourselves and our fellow humans and our environment. Well, there is no doubt that the gospel does bring us solutions to these problems, but it does so by first solving a deeper problem—the deepest of all human problems, the problem of man's relation with his Maker. And unless we make it plain that the solution of these former problems depends on the settling of this latter one, we are misrepresenting the message and becoming false witnesses of God—for a half-truth presented as if it were the whole truth becomes something of a falsehood by that very fact. No reader of the New Testament can miss the fact that it knows all about our human problems—fear, moral cowardice, illness of body and mind, loneliness, insecurity, hopelessness, despair, cruelty, abuse of power, and the rest—but equally no reader of the New Testament can miss the fact that it resolves all these problems, one way or another, into the fundamental problem of sin against God.

By sin the New Testament means not social error or failure in the first instance, but rebellion against, defiance of, retreat from, and consequent guilt before God the Creator; and sin, says the New

Testament, is the basic evil from which we need deliverance, and from which Christ died to save us. All that has gone wrong in human life between man and man is ultimately due to sin, and our present state of being in the wrong with our selves and our fellows cannot be cured as long as we remain in the wrong with God.

Space forbids us to embark here on a demonstration that the themes of sin, propitiation, and pardon are the basic structural features of the New Testament gospel, but if our readers will thoughtfully go over Romans 1–5, Galatians 3, Ephesians 1–2, Hebrews 8–10, 1 John 1–3, and the sermons in Acts, you will find that there is really no room for doubt on this point. If a query is raised on the grounds that the *word* "propitiation" appears in the New Testament only four times, the reply must be that the *thought* of propitiation appears constantly.

Sometimes the death of Christ is depicted as *reconciliation*, or peacemaking after hatred and war (Rom. 5:10–11; 2 Cor. 5:18–20; Col. 1:20–22); sometimes it is depicted as *redemption*, or rescue by ransom from danger and captivity (Rom. 3:24; Gal. 3:13; 4:5; 1 Pet. 1:18; Rev. 5:9); sometimes it is pictured as a *sacrifice* (Eph. 5:2; Heb. 9:1–10:18), an act of *self-giving* (Gal. 1:4, 2:20; 1 Tim. 2:6), *sin bearing* (John 1:29; Heb. 9:28; 1 Pet. 2:24), and *blood shedding* (Mark 14:24; Heb. 9:14; Rev. 1:5). All these thoughts have to do with the putting away of sin and the restoring of unclouded fellowship between man and God, as a glance at the texts mentioned will show; and all of them have as their background the threat of divine judgment, which Jesus' death averted. In other words, they are so many pictures and illustrations of the reality of propitiation, viewed from different standpoints. It is a shallow fallacy to imagine, as many scholars unfortunately do, that this variety of language must necessarily imply variation of thought.

A further point must now be made. Not only does the truth of propitiation lead us to the heart of the New Testament gospel, it also leads us to a vantage point from which we can see to the heart of many other things as well. When you stand on top of Mount Snowdon in Wales, you see the whole of Snowdonia spread out around you, and you have a wider view than you can get from any other point in the area. Similarly, when you are on top of the truth of propitiation, you can see the entire Bible in perspective, and you are in a position to take the measure of vital matters that cannot be properly grasped in any other terms. In what follows, five of these will be touched on: the driving force in the life of Jesus; the destiny of those who reject God; God's gift of peace; the dimensions of God's love; and the meaning of God's glory. That these matters are vital to Christianity will not be disputed. That they can be understood only in the light of the truth of propitiation cannot, we think, be denied.

The Driving Force in Jesus' Life

Think first, then, of *the driving force in the life of Jesus*.

If you sit down for an hour and read straight through the Gospel according to Mark (a very fruitful exercise: may I urge you here and now to do it), you will receive an impression of Jesus that includes at least four features.

Your basic impression will be of a man of action: a man always on the move, always altering situations and precipitating things—working miracles; calling and training disciples; upsetting error that passed as truth and irreligion that passed as godliness; and finally walking straight and open-eyed into betrayal, condemnation, and crucifixion, a freakish sequence of anomalies, which in the oddest way one is made to feel that he himself controlled all along the line.

Your further impression will be of a man who knew himself to be a divine person (Son of God) fulfilling a messianic role (Son of Man). Mark makes it clear that the more Jesus gave himself to his disciples, the more of an awesome enigma they found him—the closer they came to him, the less they understood him. This sounds paradoxical, but it was strictly true, for as their acquaintance with him deepened they were brought closer to his own understanding of himself as God and Savior, and this was something of which they could make neither head nor tail. But Jesus' unique twofold self-consciousness, confirmed by his Father's voice from heaven at his baptism and transfiguration (Mark 1:11; 9:7) came out constantly. One has only to think here of, on the one hand, the breathtaking naturalness with which he assumed absolute authority in everything he said and did (see Mark 1:22, 27; 11:27–33), and on the other hand his answer to the high priest's double question at his trial, "Are you the Christ [Messiah, God's Savior-King], the Son of the Blessed One [a supernatural and divine person]?"—to which Jesus categorically replied, "I am" (14:61–62).

Going on from this, your impression will be of One whose messianic mission centered on his being put to death—One who was consciously and singlemindedly preparing to die in this way long before the idea of a suffering Messiah took hold of anyone else. Four times at least after Peter had hailed him as the Christ at Caesarea Philippi, Jesus predicted that he would be killed and rise, though without the disciples' being able to make sense of what he said (8:31; compare vv. 34–35; 9:9, 31; 10:33–34). At other times he spoke of his being put to death as something certain (12:8; 14:18, 24), something predicted in Scripture (14:21, 49), and something that would win for many a momentously new relationship with God. "The Son of Man [came] to give his life as a ransom for many" (10:45). "This is my blood of the covenant, which is poured out for many" (14:24).

Your final impression will be of One for whom this experience of death was the most fearful ordeal. In Gethsemane, "horror and dismay came over him, and he said . . . 'My heart is ready to break with grief'" (14:34 NEB). The earnestness of his prayer (for which "he threw himself on the ground," rather than kneel or stand) was an index of the inward revulsion and desolation that he felt as he contemplated what was to come. How strong was his temptation to say "amen" after "take away this cup from me," rather than go on to "nevertheless not what I will, but what thou wilt" (14:36 KJV), we shall never know. Then, on the cross, Jesus bore witness to inward darkness matching outward darkness with his cry of dereliction, "My God, my God, why hast thou forsaken me?" (15:34 KJV).

How should we explain Jesus' belief in the necessity of his death? How should we account for the fact that what drove him on throughout his public ministry, as all four Gospels testify, was the conviction that he had to be killed? And how should we explain the fact that, whereas martyrs like Stephen faced death with joy, and even Socrates, the pagan philosopher, drank his hemlock and died without a tremor, Jesus, the perfect servant of God, who had never before showed the least fear of man or pain or loss, manifested in Gethsemane what looked like blue funk, and on the cross declared himself God-forsaken? "Never man feared death like this man," commented Luther. Why? What did it mean?

Those who see the death of Jesus as no more than a tragic accident, no different essentially from the death of any other falsely condemned good man, can make nothing of these facts at all. The only course open to them, on their principles, is to suppose that Jesus had in him a morbid, timid streak that from time to time let him down—first, inducing in him a sort of death wish, and then overwhelming him with panic and despair when death came close. But since Jesus was raised from the dead, and in the power of his risen life still taught his disciples that his death had been a necessity (Luke 24:26–27), this so-called explanation appears to be as nonsensical as it is painful. However, those who deny the truth of atonement have nothing better that they can say.

But if we relate the facts in question to the apostolic teaching about propitiation, all becomes plain at once. "May we not urge," asked James Denney, "that these experiences of deadly fear and of desertion are of one piece with the fact that in his death and in the agony of the garden through which he accepted that death as the cup which his Father gave him to drink, Jesus was taking upon him the burden of the world's sin, consenting to be, and actually being, numbered with the transgressors?"[7]

Had Paul or John been asked this question, there is no doubt what they would have answered. It was because Jesus was to be made sin, and bear God's judgment on sin, that he trembled in the

7. James Denney, *The Death of Christ* (London: Hodder and Stoughten, 1911), 46.

garden, and because he was actually bearing that judgment that he declared himself forsaken of God on the cross. The driving force in Jesus' life was his resolve to be "obedient to death—even death on a cross" (Phil. 2:8), and the unique dreadfulness of his death lies in the fact that he tasted on Calvary the wrath of God that was our due, so making propitiation for our sins.

Centuries before, Isaiah had spelled it out: "We considered him stricken by God. . . . The punishment that brought us peace was upon him. . . . The LORD has laid on him the iniquity of us all. . . . For the transgression of my people he was stricken. . . . It was the LORD's will to crush him . . . the LORD makes his life a guilt offering" (Isa. 53:4–10).

> O Christ, what burdens bowed Thy head!
> Our load was laid on Thee;
> Thou stoodest in the sinner's stead,
> Didst bear all ill for me.
> A victim led, Thy blood was shed;
> Now there's no load for me.
>
> The Holy One did hide His face;
> O Christ, 'twas hid from Thee:
> Dumb darkness wrapped Thy soul a space,
> The darkness due to me.
> But now that face of radiant grace
> Shines forth in light on me.

We have been full on this, because of its importance for understanding the basic Christian facts; the next sections can be shorter.

What of Those Who Reject God?

Think, second, of *the destiny of those who reject God.*

Universalists suppose that the class of people mentioned in this heading will ultimately have no members, but the Bible indicates otherwise. Decisions made in this life will have eternal consequences. "Do not be deceived" (as you would be if you listened to the universalists); "God cannot be mocked. A man reaps what he sows"

(Gal. 6:7). Those who in this life reject God will forever be rejected by God. Universalism is the doctrine that, among others, Judas will be saved, but Jesus did not think he would. "The Son of Man will go just as it is written about him. But woe to that man who betrays the Son of Man! It would be better for him if he had not been born" (Mark 14:21). How could Jesus have spoken those last words if he had expected Judas finally to be saved?

Some, then, face an eternity of rejectedness. How can we understand what they will bring on themselves? We cannot, of course, form any adequate notion of hell, any more than we can of heaven, and no doubt it is good for us that this is so; but perhaps the clearest notion we can form is that derived from contemplating the cross.

On the cross, God judged our sins in the person of his Son, and Jesus endured the retributive comeback of our wrongdoing. Look at the cross, therefore, and you see what form God's judicial reaction to human sin will finally take. What form is that? In a word, withdrawal and deprivation of good. On the cross Jesus lost all the good that he had before: all sense of his Father's presence and love, all sense of physical, mental, and spiritual well-being, all enjoyment of God and of created things, all ease and solace of friendship, were taken from him, and in their place was nothing but loneliness, pain, a killing sense of human malice and callousness, and a horror of great spiritual darkness.

The physical pain, though great (for crucifixion remains the cruelest form of judicial execution that the world has ever known), was yet only a small part of the story; Jesus' chief sufferings were mental and spiritual, and what was packed into less than four hundred minutes was an eternity of agony—agony such that each minute was an eternity in itself, as mental sufferers know that individual minutes can be.

So, too, those who reject God face the prospect of losing all good, and the best way to form an idea of eternal death is to dwell on this thought. In ordinary life, we never notice how much good we enjoy through God's common grace till it is taken from us. We never value health, or steady circumstances, or friendship and respect from others, as we should till we have lost them. Calvary shows that under the final judgment of God nothing that one has valued, or could value, nothing that one can call good, remains to one. It is a terrible thought, but the reality, we may be sure, is more terrible yet. "It would be better for him if he had not been born." God help us to learn this lesson, which the spectacle of propitiation through penal substitution on the cross teaches so clearly; and may each of us be found in Christ, our sins covered by his blood, at the last.

What Is Peace?

Think, third, of *God's gift of peace.*

What does the gospel of God offer us? If we say "the peace of God," none will demur—but will everyone understand? The use of right words does not guarantee right thoughts! Too often the peace of God is thought of as if it were essentially a feeling of inner tranquility, happy and carefree, springing from knowledge that God will shield one from life's hardest knocks. But this is a misrepresentation, for, on the one hand, God does not featherbed his children in this way, and anyone who thinks he does is in for a shock, and, on the other hand, that which is basic and essential to the real peace of God does not come into this concept at all.

The truths, after which this account of God's peace is feeling (though it misrepresents them, as we said) is that God's peace brings us two things: both power to face and live with our own badness and failings, and also contentment under "the slings and arrows of outrageous fortune" (for which the Christian name is God's wise providence). The truth that this account ignores is that the basic ingredient in God's peace, without which the rest cannot be, is pardon and acceptance into covenant—that is, adoption into God's family. But where this change of relationship with God—out of hostility into friendship, out of wrath into the fullness of love, out of condemnation into justification—is not set forth, the gospel of peace is not truly set forth either.

The peace *of* God is first and foremost peace *with* God; it is the state of affairs in which God, instead of being *against* us, is *for* us. No account of God's peace that does not start here can do other than mislead. One of the miserable ironies of our time is that whereas liberal and radical theologians believe themselves to be restating the gospel for today, they have for the most part rejected the categories of wrath, guilt, condemnation, and the enmity of God, and so have made it impossible for themselves ever to present the gospel at all, for they cannot now state the basic problem that the gospel of peace solves.

The peace of God, then, primarily and fundamentally, is a new relationship of forgiveness and acceptance—and the source from which it flows is propitiation. When Jesus came to his disciples in the upper room at evening on his resurrection day, he said, "Peace be with you"; and when he had said that, "he showed unto them his hands and side" (John 20:19–20 PHILLIPS). Why did he do that? Not just to establish his identity, but to remind them of the propitiatory death on the cross whereby he had made peace with his Father for them. Having suffered in their place, as their substitute, to make peace for them, he now came in his risen power to bring that peace to them.

"Look, the Lamb of God, who takes away the sin of the world!" (John 1:29). It is here, in the recognition that, whereas we are by nature at odds with God, and God with us, Jesus has made "peace through his blood shed on the cross" (Col. 1:20), that true knowledge of the peace of God begins.

The Dimensions of God's Love

Think, fourth, of *the dimensions of the love of God*.

Paul prays that the readers of his Ephesian letter "may have power, together with all the saints, to grasp how wide and long and high and deep is the love of Christ, and to know this love that surpasses knowledge" (Eph. 3:18–19). The touch of incoherence and paradox in his language reflects Paul's sense that the reality of divine love is inexpressibly great; nevertheless, he believes that some comprehension of it can be reached. How?

The answer of Ephesians is, by considering propitiation in its context—that is, by reviewing the whole plan of grace set forth in the first two chapters of the letter (election, redemption, regeneration, preservation, glorification), of which plan the atoning sacrifice of Christ is the centerpiece. See the key references to redemption and "remission of sins" and the bringing near to God of those who were far off, through the *blood* (sacrificial death) of Christ. (1:7; 2:13). See also the teaching of chapter 5, which twice points to Christ's propitiatory sacrifice of himself on our behalf as the demonstration and measure of his love for us, the love that we are to imitate in our dealings with each other. "Live a life of love, just as Christ loved us and gave himself up for us as a fragrant offering and sacrifice to God" (5:2). "Husbands, love your wives, just as Christ loved the church and gave himself up for her" (5:25).

Christ's love was *free*, not elicited by any goodness in us (2:1–5); it was *eternal*, being one with the choice of sinners to save that the Father made "before the foundation of the world" (1:4 ESV); it was *unreserved*, for it led him down to the depths of humiliation and, indeed, of hell itself on Calvary; and it was *sovereign*, for it has achieved its object—the final glory of the redeemed, their perfect holiness and happiness in the fruition of his love (5:26–27), is now guaranteed and assured (1:14; 2:7–10; 4:11–16, 30). Dwell on these things, Paul urges, if you would catch a sight, however dim, of the greatness and the glory of divine love. It is these things that make up "his glorious grace" (1:6 ESV); only those who know them can praise the name of the triune Jehovah as they should. Which brings us to our last point.

The Glory of God

Think, lastly, of *the meaning of God's glory*.

In the upper room, after Judas had gone out into the night to betray him, Jesus said, "Now is the Son of Man glorified and God is glorified in him" (John 13:31). What did he mean? "Son of Man" was his name for himself as the Savior-King who before being enthroned must fulfill Isaiah 53; and when he spoke of the present glorifying of the Son of Man, and of God in him, he was thinking specifically of the atoning death, the "lifting up" on the cross, which Judas had gone to precipitate. Do you see the glory of God in his wisdom, power, righteousness, truth, and love, supremely disclosed at Calvary, in the making of propitiation for our sins? The Bible does; and we venture to add, if you felt the burden and pressure of your own sins at their true weight, so would you.

In heaven, where these things are better understood, angels and men unite to praise "the Lamb, who was slain" (Rev. 5:12; see 7:9–12). Here on earth those who by grace have been made spiritual realists do the same.

> Bearing shame and scoffing rude
> In my place condemned He stood;
> Sealed my pardon with His blood:
> Hallelujah! What a Saviour! . . .

> He left His Father's throne above,
> So free, so infinite His grace;
> Emptied Himself of all but love
> And bled for Adam's helpless race.
> Amazing Love! How can it be?
> For O, my God, it found out me! . . .

> If Thou hast my discharge procured,
> And freely in my room endured
> The whole of wrath divine,
> Payment God cannot twice demand,
> First at my bleeding Surety's hand,
> And then again at mine.

> Turn then, my soul, unto they rest;
> The merits of thy great High Priest
> Have bought thy liberty.

51

Trust in His efficacious blood,
Nor fear thy banishment from God,
  Since Jesus died for thee!

These are the songs of the heirs of heaven, those who have seen "the light of the knowledge of the glory of God in the face [that is, the person, office, and achievement] of Christ" (2 Cor. 4:6). The joyful news of redeeming love and propitiating mercy, which is the heart of the gospel, spurs them to never-ending praise. Are you among their number?

2

What Did the Cross Achieve?

The Logic of Penal Substitution

J. I. Packer

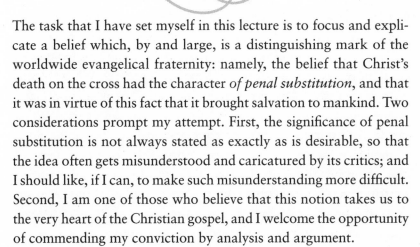

The task that I have set myself in this lecture is to focus and explicate a belief which, by and large, is a distinguishing mark of the
worldwide evangelical fraternity: namely, the belief that Christ's
death on the cross had the character *of penal substitution*, and that
it was in virtue of this fact that it brought salvation to mankind. Two
considerations prompt my attempt. First, the significance of penal
substitution is not always stated as exactly as is desirable, so that
the idea often gets misunderstood and caricatured by its critics; and
I should like, if I can, to make such misunderstanding more difficult.
Second, I am one of those who believe that this notion takes us to
the very heart of the Christian gospel, and I welcome the opportunity
of commending my conviction by analysis and argument.

My plan is this: first, to clear up some questions of method, so
that there will be no doubt as to what I am doing; second, to explore
what it means to call Christ's death *substitutionary*; third, to see what
further meaning is added when Christ's substitutionary suffering
is called *penal*; fourth, to note in closing that the analysis offered

is not out of harmony with learned exegetical opinion. These are, I believe, needful preliminaries to any serious theological estimate of this view.

Mystery and Model

Every theological question has behind it a history of study, and narrow eccentricity in handling it is unavoidable unless the history is taken into account. Adverse comment on the concept of penal substitution often betrays narrow eccentricity of this kind. The two main historical points relating to this idea are, first, that Luther, Calvin, Zwingli, Melanchthon, and their reforming contemporaries were the pioneers in stating it and, second, that the arguments brought against it in 1578 by the Unitarian Pelagian Faustus Socinus in his brilliant polemic *De Jesu Christo Servatore* (*Of Jesus Christ the Savior*)[1] have been central in discussion of it ever since. What the Reformers did was to redefine *satisfactio* (satisfaction), the main medieval category for thought about the cross. Anselm's *Cur Deus Homo?* which largely determined the medieval development, saw Christ's *satisfactio* for our sins as the offering of compensation or damages for dishonor done, but the Reformers saw it as the undergoing of vicarious punishment (*poena*) to meet the claims on us of God's holy law and wrath (i.e., his punitive justice). What Socinus did was to arraign this idea as irrational, incoherent, immoral, and impossible. Giving pardon, he argued, does not square with taking satisfaction, nor does the transferring of punishment from the guilty to the innocent square with justice; nor is the temporary death of one a true substitute for the eternal death of many; and a perfect substitutionary satisfaction, could such a thing be, would necessarily confer on us unlimited permission to continue in sin. Socinus's alternative account of New Testament soteriology, based on the axiom that God forgives without requiring any satisfaction save the

1. Socinus's arguments were incorporated in the *Racovian Catechism*, published at Racow (the modern Cracow) in 1605, which set forth the Unitarianism of the "Polish Brethren." After several revisions of detail down to 1680 the text was finalized and in due course translated into English by Thomas Rees (London, 1818). It is a document of classical importance in Unitarian history.

repentance that makes us forgivable, was evasive and unconvincing and had little influence. But his classic critique proved momentous: it held the attention of all exponents of the Reformation view for more than a century and created a tradition of rationalistic prejudice against that view that has effectively shaped debate about it right down to our own day.

The almost mesmeric effect of Socinus's critique on Reformed scholastics in particular was on the whole unhappy. It forced them to develop rational strength in stating and connecting up the various parts of their position, which was good, but it also led them to fight back on the challenger's own ground, using the Socinian technique of arguing *a priori* about God as if he were a man—to be precise, a sixteenth- or seventeenth-century monarch, head of both the legislature and the judiciary in his own realm but bound nonetheless to respect existing law and judicial practice at every point. So the God of Calvary came to be presented in a whole series of expositions right down to that of Louis Berkhof (1938) as successfully avoiding all the moral and legal lapses which Socinus claimed to find in the Reformation view.[2] But these demonstrations, however skillfully done (and demonstrators like Francis Turretin and A. A. Hodge, to name but two,[3] were very skillful indeed), had built-in weaknesses. Their stance was defensive rather than declaratory, analytical and apologetic rather than doxological and kerygmatic. They made the word of the cross sound more like a conundrum than a confession of faith—more like a puzzle, we might say, than a gospel. What was happening? Just this: that in trying to beat Socinian rationalism at its own game, Reformed theologians were conceding the Socinian assumption that every aspect of God's work of reconciliation will be exhaustively explicable

2. See L. Berkhof, *Systematic Theology* (Grand Rapids, MI: Eerdmans; London: Banner of Truth, 1949), 373–83. Berkhof's zeal to show that God did nothing illegal or unjust makes a strange impression on the post-Watergate reader.

3. See F. Turretin, *Institutio Theologiae Elenchticae* (Geneva, 1682), 2:xiv, "De Officio Christi Mediatoris," and A. A. Hodge, *The Atonement* (London: Nelson, 1868). Turretin's position is usefully summarized in L. W. Grensted, *A Short History of the Doctrine of the Atonement* (Manchester: Manchester University Press, 1920), 241–52. Cf. J. F. Heidegger's parallel account in his *Corpus Theologiae Christianae* (Zurich, 1700), which R. S. Franks reviews in *The Work of Christ* (London: Nelson, 1962), 426ff.

in terms of a natural theology of divine government, drawn from the world of contemporary legal and political thought. Thus, in their zeal to show themselves rational, they became rationalistic.[4] Here as elsewhere, methodological rationalism became in the seventeenth century a worm in the Reformed bud, leading in the next two centuries to a large-scale withering of its theological flower.

Now I do not query the substantial rightness of the Reformed view of the atonement; on the contrary, I hope to confirm it, as will appear; but I think it is vital that we should unambiguously renounce any such intellectual method as that which I have described and look for a better one. I shall now try to commend what seems to me a sounder method by offering answers to two questions: (1) What sort of knowledge of Christ's achievement on the cross is open to us? (2) From what source and by what means do we gain it?

(1) What sort of knowledge of God's action in Christ's death may we have? That a man named Jesus was crucified under Pontius Pilate about A.D. 30 is common historical knowledge, but Christian beliefs about his divine identity and the significance of his dying cannot be deduced from that fact alone. What further sort of knowledge about the cross, then, may Christians enjoy?

4. In his influential book *Christus Victor*, trans. A. G. Hebert (London: SPCK, 1931), which advocated a "dramatic," nonrational way of declaring God's conquest of evil through the cross, Gustaf Aulén describes the "Latin" account of the atonement (i.e., that of Anselm and Protestant orthodoxy) as "juridical in its inmost essence" (p. 106), and says:

> It concentrates its effort upon a rational attempt to explain how the Divine Love and the Divine Justice can be reconciled. The Love of God is regulated by His Justice, and is only free to act within the limits that Justice marks out. *Ratio* and *Lex*, rationality and justice, go hand in hand. . . . The attempt is made by the scholastics to elaborate a theology which shall provide a comprehensive explanation of the Divine government of the world, which shall answer all questions and solve all riddles. (173f.)

What Aulén fails to note is how much of this implicitly rationalistic cast of thought was a direct reaction to Socinus's rationalistic critique. In fact, Aulén does not mention Socinus at all; nor does he refer to Calvin, who asserts penal substitution as strongly as any, but follows an exegetical and Christocentric method that is not in the least scholastic or rationalistic. Calvin shows no interest in the reconciling of God's love and justice as a theoretical problem; his only interest is in the mysterious but blessed fact that at the cross God did act in both love and justice to save us from our sins. Cf. P. van Buren, *Christ in Our Place: The Substitutionary Character of Calvin's Doctrine of Reconciliation* (Edinburgh: Oliver and Boyd, 1957).

The answer, we may say, is *faith-knowledge*: by faith we know that God was in Christ reconciling the world to himself. Yes, indeed; but what sort of knowledge is faith-knowledge? It is a kind of knowledge of which God is both giver and content. It is a Spirit-given acquaintance with divine realities, given through acquaintance with God's Word. It is a kind of knowledge that makes the knower say in one and the same breath both "whereas I was blind, now I see" (John 9:25 KJV) and also "now we see in a mirror, darkly . . . now I know in part" (1 Cor. 13:12 ESV). For it is a unique kind of knowledge that, though real, is not full; it is knowledge of what is discernible within a circle of light against the background of a larger darkness; it is, in short, knowledge of a *mystery*, the mystery of the living God at work.

"Mystery" is used here as it was by Charles Wesley when he wrote:

> 'Tis *mystery* all! The immortal dies!
> Who can explore his strange design?
> In vain the first-born seraph tries
> To sound the depths of love divine!

"Mystery" in this sense (traditional in theology) means a reality distinct from us that in our very apprehending of it remains unfathomable to us: a reality which we acknowledge as actual without knowing how it is possible, and which we therefore describe as *incomprehensible*. Christian metaphysicians, moved by wonder at the world, speak of the created order as *mystery*, meaning that there is more to it, and more of God in it, than they can grasp; and similarly Christian theologians, taught by revelation, apply the same word for parallel reasons to the self-revealed and self-revealing God and to his work of reconciliation and redemption through Christ. It will be seen that this definition of mystery corresponds less to Paul's use of the word μυστήριον (which he applied to the open secret of God's saving purpose, set forth in the gospel) than to his prayer that the Ephesians might "know the love of Christ *that surpasses knowledge*" (Eph. 3:19 ESV). Knowing through divine enlightenment that which passes knowledge is precisely what it means to be acquainted with the mystery of God. The revealed "mystery" (in Paul's sense) of Christ confronts us with the unfathomable "mystery" (in the sense I defined) of the Creator who exceeds the comprehension of his creatures. Accordingly, Paul ends his full-dress, richest-ever exposition of the mystery of Christ by crying: "O depth of wealth, wisdom, and knowledge in God! How unsearchable his judgments, how untraceable his ways! Who knows the mind of the Lord? . . . Source, Guide and Goal of all that is—to him to be glory for ever! Amen" (Rom. 11:33ff. NEB). Here Paul shows, and shares, his awareness that the God of Jesus remains the God of Job, and that the highest wisdom of the theological theorist, even when working under divine inspiration as Paul did, is to recognize that he is, as it were, gazing into the sun, whose very brightness makes it impossible for him fully to see it; so that at the end of the day he has to admit that God is much more to him than theories can ever contain, and to humble himself in adoration before the one whom he can never fully analyze.

Now the atonement is a mystery in the defined sense, one aspect of the total mystery of God. But it does not stand alone in this. Every aspect of God's reality and work, without exception, is mystery. The eternal Trinity; God's sovereignty in creation, providence, and grace; the incarnation, exaltation, present reign, and approaching return of Jesus Christ; the inspiring of the Holy Scriptures; and the ministry of the Spirit in the Christian and the church—each of these (to look no further) is a reality beyond our full fathoming, just as the cross is. And theories about any of these things that used human analogies to dispel the dimension of mystery would deserve our distrust, just as rationalistic theories about the cross do.

It must be stressed that the mystery is in each case the reality itself, as distinct from anything in our apprehension of it, and as distinct therefore from our theories, problems, affirmations, and denials about it. What makes it a mystery is that creatures like ourselves can comprehend it only in part. To say this does not open the door to skepticism, for our knowledge of divine realities (like our knowledge of each other) is genuine knowledge expressed in notions which, so far as they go, are true. But it does close the door against rationalism, in the sense of theorizing that claims to explain with finality any aspect of God's way of existing and working. And with that, it alerts us to the fact that the presence in our theology of unsolved problems is not necessarily a reflection on the truth or adequacy of our thoughts. Inadequate and untrue theories do of course exist: a theory (the word comes from θεωρεῖν, "to look at") is a "view" or "sight" of something, and if one's way of looking at it is perverse one's view will be distorted, and distorted views are always full of problems. But the mere presence of problems is not enough to prove a view distorted; true views in theology also entail unsolved problems, while any view that was problem-free would certainly be rationalistic and reductionist. True theories in theology, whether about the atonement or anything else, will suspect themselves of being inadequate to their object throughout. One thing that Christians know by faith is that they know only in part.

None of this, of course, is new or unfamiliar; it all belongs to the main historic stream of Christian thought. But I state it here, perhaps too laboriously, because it has not always been brought to bear rigorously enough on the doctrine of the atonement. Also, this position has linguistic implications that touch the doctrine of the atonement in ways that are not always fully grasped; and my next task is to show what these are.

Human knowledge and thoughts are expressed in words, and what we must note now is that all attempts to speak of the mystery of the unique and transcendent God involve many kinds of *stretching* of ordinary language. We say, for instance, that God is both plural and singular, being three in one; that he directs and determines the free acts of men; that he is wise, good, and sovereign, when he allows Christians to starve or die of cancer; that the divine Son has always upheld the universe, even when he was a human baby; and so forth. At first sight, such statements might appear nonsensical (either meaningless or false). But Christians say that, though they would be nonsensical if made of men, they are true as statements about God. If so, however, it is clear that the key words are not being used in an everyday way.

Whatever our views on the origins of human language and the inspiration of the Scriptures (both matters on which it seems that options are currently being broadened rather than reduced), there can be no dispute that the meaning of all the nouns, adjectives, and verbs that we use for stating facts and giving descriptions is anchored, at least in the first instance, in our experience of knowing things and people (ourselves included) in this world. Ordinary language is thus being adapted for an extraordinary purpose when we use it to speak of God. Christians have always made this adaptation easily in their prayers, praises, and proclamations, as if it were a natural thing to do (as indeed I think it is), and the doubts articulated by living if somewhat old-fashioned philosophers like A. J. Ayer and Antony Flew as to whether such utterance expresses knowledge and conveys information about anything more than private attitudes seem curiously provincial as well as paradoxical.[5]

Moreover, it is noticeable that the common Christian verbal forms for expressing divine mysteries have from the first shown remarkable consistency and steadiness in maintaining their built-in logical strangeness, as if the apprehended reality of God was itself sustaining them (as indeed I think it was). Language about the cross illustrates this clearly: liturgies, hymns, and literature, homiletical, catechetical, and apologetic, all show that Christians have from the start lived by faith in Christ's death as a sacrifice made to God in reparation for their sins, however uncouth and mythological such talk sounds (and must always have sounded), however varied the presentations of atonement that teachers tried out, and however little actual the-

---

5. Ayer voiced his doubts in *Language, Truth and Logic* (London: Gollancz, 1936; 2nd ed. 1946); Flew, his in "Theology and Falsification," *New Essays in Philosophical Theology*, ed. A. G. N. Flew and Alasdair MacIntyre, (London: SCM, 1955), 96–130. There are replies in, among other books, E. L. Mascall, *Words and Images* (London: Longmans, 1957); *Faith and Logic*, ed. Basil Mitchell (London: Allen and Unwin, 1957); Frederick Ferré, *Language, Logic and God* (London: Eyre and Spottiswoode, 1962; Fontana ed. 1970); W. Hordern, *Speaking of God* (New York: Macmillan, 1964).

ologizing about the cross went on in particular periods, especially the early centuries.[6]

Christian language, with its peculiarities, has been much studied during the past twenty years, and two things about it have become clear. First, all its odd, "stretched," contradictory- and incoherent-sounding features derive directly from the unique Christian notion of the transcendent, tripersonal Creator-God. Christians regard God as free from the limits that bind creatures like ourselves, who bear God's image while not existing on his level, and Christian language, following biblical precedent, shakes free from ordinary limits in a way that reflects this fact. So, for instance, faced with John's declaration in 1 John 4:8–10 (KJV), "God is love. . . . Herein is love, not that we loved God, but that he loved us, and sent his Son to be the propitiation for our sins," Calvin can write without hesitation: "The word propitiation (*placatio*; Greek, ἱλασμος) has great weight: for God, in a way that cannot be put into words (*ineffabili quodam modo*), at the very time when he loved us, was hostile (*infensus*) to us till he was reconciled in Christ."[7] Calvin's phrase "in a way that cannot be put into words" is his acknowledgement that the mystery of God is beyond our grasp. To Calvin, this duality of attitude, love and hostility, which in human psychological terms is inconceivable, is part of God's moral glory, a sentiment that might make rationalistic theologians shake their heads, but at which John certainly would have nodded his.

Second, Christian speech verbalizes the apprehended mystery of God by using a distinctive non-representational "picture-language."

6. Of the church in the patristic period H. E. W. Turner writes: "Its experience of Redemption through Christ was far richer than its attempted formulations of this experience." *The Patristic Doctrine of Redemption* (London: Mowbray, 1952), 13; cf. chap. 5, "Christ Our Victim." On T. F. Torrance's sharp-edged thesis in *The Doctrine of Grace in the Apostolic Fathers* (Edinburgh: Oliver and Boyd, 1948) that the apostolic Fathers lapsed from New Testament faith in the cross to a legalism of self-salvation, Robert S. Paul's comment in *The Atonement and the Sacraments* (London: Hodder and Stoughton, 1961), 37, note 2, is just: "To me he has made his case almost too well, for at the end I am left asking the question, 'In what sense, then, could the Church change this much and still be the Church?'" In fact, Torrance's thesis needs the qualification of Turner's statement quoted above.

7. *Inst.* 2:xvii. 2. This thought is picked up in Anglican Article II: "Christ . . . truly suffered . . . *to reconcile his Father to us*, and to be a sacrifice, not only for original guilt, but also for all actual sins of men." On propitiation, cf. note 21 below.

This consists of parables, analogies, metaphors, and images piled up in balance with each other, as in the Bible itself (from which this language is first learned), and all pointing to the reality of God's presence and action in order to evoke awareness of it and response to it. Analysis of the functioning of this language is currently in full swing,[8] and no doubt much remains to be said. Already, however, the discussion has produced one firm result of major importance—the recognition that the verbal units of Christian speech are "models," comparable to the thought-models of modern physics.[9] The significance of this appears from John MacIntyre's judgment "that the theory of models succeeds in reinstating the doctrine of analogy in modern theological logic . . . and that analogy is to be interpreted in terms of a theory of models and not *vice versa.*"[10]

The doctrine of analogy is the time-harbored account, going back to Aquinas, of how ordinary language is used to speak intelligibly of a God who is partly like us (because we bear his image) and partly unlike us (because he is the infinite Creator while we are finite creatures).[11] All theological models, like the nondescriptive models of the physical sciences, have an analogical character; they are, we might say, analogies with a purpose, thought-patterns that

8. For surveys of the present state of play, see Ferré's *Language, Logic and God*; Ian G. Barbour, *Myths, Models and Paradigms* (London: SCM, 1974); John Macquarrie, *God-Talk* (London: SCM, 1967).

9. The pioneer in stating this was Ian T. Ramsey. See his *Religious Language* (London: SCM, 1957); *Models and Mystery* (London: Oxford University Press, 1964); *Christian Discourse* (London: Oxford University Press, 1965). For further discussion of models in theology, cf. John MacIntyre, *The Shape of Christology* (London: SCM, 1966), esp. 54–81; Thomas Fawcett, *The Symbolic Language of Religion* (London: SCM, 1970), 69–94; Barbour, *op. cit.*

10. John MacIntyre, *The Shape of Christology*, 63.

11. The idea of analogy is formulated by the *Oxford Dictionary of the Christian Church*, s.v., as follows: "A method of predication whereby concepts derived from a familiar object are made applicable to a relatively unknown object in virtue of some similarity between the two otherwise dissimilar objects." Aquinas's account of analogy is in *Summa Theologica* 1:xiii and can be read in Ian T. Ramsey, ed., *Words about God*, (London: SCM, 1971), 36ff.

For Thomists, the doctrine of analogy serves to explain how knowledge of creatures gives knowledge of their Creator (natural theology) as well as how biblical imagery gives knowledge of the God of both nature and grace (scriptural theology). For a technical Thomist discussion concentrating on analogy in natural theology, see E. L. Mascall, *Existence and Analogy* (London: Longmans, 1949), 92–121.

function in a particular way, teaching us to focus one area of reality (relationships with God) by conceiving of it in terms of another, better known area of reality (relationships with each other). Thus they actually inform us about our relationship with God and through the Holy Spirit enable us to unify, clarify, and intensify our experience in that relationship.

The last song in *Joseph and the Amazing Technicolor Dreamcoat* assures us that "any dream will do" to wake the weary into joy. Will any model do to give knowledge of the living God? Historically, Christians have not thought so. Their characteristic theological method, whether practiced clumsily or skillfully, consistently or inconsistently, has been to take biblical models as their God-given starting point, to base their belief system on what biblical writers use these models to say, and to let these models operate as "controls," both suggesting and delimiting what further, secondary models may be developed in order to explicate these that are primary. As models in physics are hypotheses formed under the suggestive control of empirical evidence to correlate and predict phenomena, so Christian theological models are explanatory constructs formed to help us know, understand, and deal with God, the ultimate reality.

From this standpoint, the whole study of Christian theology—biblical, historical, and systematic—is the exploring of a three-tier hierarchy of models: first, the "control" models given in Scripture (God, Son of God, kingdom of God, Word of God, love of God, glory of God, body of Christ, justification, adoption, redemption, new birth, and so forth—in short, all the concepts analyzed in Kittel's great *Wörterbuch* and its many epigoni); next, dogmatic models that the church crystallized out to define and defend the faith (homoousion, Trinity, nature, hypostatic union, double procession, sacrament, supernatural, etc.—in short, all the concepts usually dealt with in doctrinal textbooks); finally, interpretive models lying between Scripture and defined dogma that particular theologians and theological schools developed for stating the faith to contemporaries (penal substitution, verbal inspiration, divinization, Barth's "Nihil"—*das Nichtige*—and many more).

It is helpful to think of theology in these terms, and of the atonement in particular. Socinus went wrong in this matter first by identifying the biblical model of God's kingship with his own sixteenth-century monarchy model (a mistake later repeated by Hugo Grotius); second, by treating this not-wholly-biblical model as his "control"; and third, by failing to acknowledge that the mystery of God is more than any one model, even the best, can express. We have already noticed that some orthodox writers answering Socinus tended to slip in a similar way. The passion to pack God into a conceptual box of our own making is always strong but must be resisted. If we bear in mind that all the knowledge we can have of the atonement is of a mystery about which we can only think and speak by means of models, and which remains a mystery when all is said and done, it will keep us from rationalistic pitfalls and thus help our progress considerably.

Bible and Model

Now we come up to our second question, my answer to which has been hinted at already. By what means is knowledge of the mystery of the cross given us? I reply: through the didactic thought-models given in the Bible, which in truth are instruction from God. In other words, I proceed on the basis of the mainstream Christian belief in biblical inspiration, which I have sought to justify elsewhere.[12]

What this belief means, in formula terms, is that the Holy Scriptures of both Testaments have the dual character that the *viva voce* teaching of prophets, apostles, and supremely Jesus had: in content, if not in grammatical form, it is both human witness to God and God's witness to himself. The true analogy for inspiration is incarnation, the personal Word of God becoming flesh. As a multiple confession of faith in the God who rules, judges, and saves in the space-time continuum that we call world history, the Bible consists of occasional documents—historical, didactic and liturgical—all proclaiming in various ways what God has done, is doing, and will

---

12. See my *"Fundamentalism" and the Word of God* (London: IVF, 1958); *God Has Spoken* (London: Hodder and Stoughton, 1965); "Inspiration," in *The New Bible Dictionary*, ed. J. D. Douglas, et al. (London: IVF, 1962).

do. Each document and each utterance within that document, like Jesus Christ and each of his utterances, is anchored in a particular historical situation—this particularity marks all the Christian revelation—and to discern within these particularities truths from God for universal application is the interpreter's major task. His guideline is the knowledge that God's word for today is found through understanding and reapplying the word that God spoke long ago in identity (substantial, not grammatical) with the message of the biblical authors. The way into God's mind remains via their minds, for their assertions about God embody in particularized form what he wants to tell us today about himself.

In other words, God *says* in application to us the same things that he originally *said* in application to those to whom the biblical books were first addressed. The details of the second application differ from the first in a way that corresponds to the difference between our situation and that of the first addressees, but the truths of principle being applied are the same. Divine speech is itself, of course, a model, but it is a controlling one. It signifies the reality of mind-to-mind instruction from God to us by verbal means, and thus teaches us to categorize all other didactic models found in Scripture, not as hypothesis or hunch, but as revelation.

How do these revealed models become means of God's instruction? Here, it must regretfully be said, Ian Ramsey, the pioneer exponent of the model-structure of biblical thinking, fails us. He describes vividly how these models trigger off religious disclosures and so evoke religious responses, but instead of equating the beliefs they express with divine teaching, he leaves quite open, and therefore quite obscure, the relation between the "disclosures" as intuitions of reality and the thoughts that the models convey. This means that he lacks criteria for distinguishing true from false intuitions. Sometimes he speaks as if all feelings of "cosmic disclosure" convey insights that are true and self-authenticating, but one need only mention the Buddha, Mohammed, Mrs. Mary Baker Eddy, the false prophets exposed by Jeremiah, Ezekiel, and Micaiah in 1 Kings 22, and the visionaries of Colossians 2:18f. to show that this is not so. Also Ramsey seems to be without criteria for relating models to each other and developing from them a coherent belief-system, and he nowhere considers what the divine-speech model implies.[13]

Must our understanding of how biblical models function be as limited or as loose as Ramsey's is? Not necessarily. Recognition that the biblical witness to God has the logic of models—not isolated, incidentally, but linked together, and qualifying each other in sizeable units of meaning—is compatible with all the views taken in the modern hermeneutical debate. Central to this debate are two questions. The first is whether the reference point and subject matter of biblical witness is just the transformed psyche, the "new being" as such, or whether it does not also, and indeed primarily, refer to saving acts of God and a living divine Savior that were originally "there" as datable realities in the space-time continuum of world history, and that owe their transforming power "here" in Christian lives now to the fact that they were "there" on the stage of history then. To the extent that the former alternative is embraced, one has to say that the only factual information that the biblical writers

13. For Ramsey's overall view of models, see the works cited in note 9. On most theological subjects his opinions, so far as he reveals them, are unexceptionably middle-of-the-road, but it is noteworthy that in his lecture "Atonement Theology" in *Christian Discourse* (pp. 28ff.) he hails Hastings Rashdall's Abelardian treatise *The Idea of Atonement in Christian Theology* (1919) as "definitive" (p. 29; no reasons given); limits the "cosmic disclosure" evoked by the cross to a sense of "the victorious will of God," whose plan to maintain a remnant did not fail (pp. 32, 34), and whose love this victory shows (pp. 59f.); rejects the grounding of justification on substitution or satisfaction as involving "frontier-clashes with the language of morals" (p. 40; the old Socinian objection); and criticizes the exegeting of justification, substitution, satisfaction, reconciliation, redemption, propitiation, and expiation as if these words "were *not models at all,* but described procedural transactions . . . each describing a species of atonement engineering" (p. 44). Profound confusion appears here. Certainly these words are models, but what they are models of is precisely procedural transactions for achieving atonement, transactions in which the Father and the Son dealt with each other on our behalf. The contexts of apostolic argument in which these models appear make this unambiguously plain, and to assume, as Ramsey seems to do, that as models they can only have a directly subjective reference to what Bultmann would call a new self-understanding is quite arbitrary. Indeed, Ramsey himself goes on to show that the model-category for biblical concepts does *not* require an exclusively subjective reference, for he dwells on "love" as a model of *God's activity* (p. 59); and if love can be such a model, why not these other words? It seems evident that Ramsey brought Abelardian-Socinian assumptions to his study of the biblical words, rather than deriving his views from that study.

communicate is that God's people felt and thought in certain ways at certain times in certain situations. Then one has to face the question whether the writers thought this was all the factual information they were communicating; if one says no, then one has to justify one's disagreement with them; if one says yes, one has to explain why so much of their witness to Christ has the form of factual narration about him—why, indeed, the "gospel" as a literary form was ever invented.

If, however, one takes the latter alternative, as all sober reason seems to counsel, then the second central question arises: how much distortion of fact is there in the narrating, and how much of guess-work, hunch, and fantasy is there in the interpreting of the histori-cal realities that were "there"? I cannot discuss these massive and complex issues here; suffice it to declare, in relation to this debate, that I am proceeding on the basis that the biblical writers do indeed give true information about certain historical events, public and in principle datable, that have resulted in a Savior and a salvation being "there" for sinners to receive by faith; and that the biblical thought-models in terms of which these events are presented and explained are *revealed* models, ways of thought that God himself has taught us for the true understanding of what he has done *for* us and will do *in* us.

Also, I proceed on the basis that the Holy Spirit, who inspired prophetic and apostolic testimony in its written as well as its oral form, is now active to teach Christians through it, making them aware of its divine quality overall, its message to themselves, and the presence and potency of God in Christ to whom it points. Since the Spirit has been teaching the church in this way in every age, much of our listening to the Bible in the present will rightly take the form of reviewing theological constructions of the past, testing them by the written word from which they took their rise. When a particular theological view, professedly Bible-based, has over the centuries proved a mainspring of Christian devotion, faith, and love, one approaches it, not indeed uncritically, but with respect, antici-pating the discovery that it is substantially right. Our present task is to elucidate and evaluate one historic line of biblical interpretation that has had an incalculable impact on countless lives since it was clarified in the century of the Reformation; it will be strange if it proves to have been entirely wrong.[14]

So much, then, for methodological preliminaries, which have been tedious but necessary; now to our theme directly.

Substitution

The first thing to say about penal substitution has been said already. It is a Christian theological model, based on biblical exegesis, formed to focus a particular awareness of what Jesus did at Calvary to bring us to God. If we wish to speak of the "doctrine" of penal substitution, we should remember that this model is a dramatic, kerygmatic picturing of divine action, much more like Aulén's "classic idea" of divine victory (though Aulén never saw this) than it is like the defensive formula-models that we call the Nicene "doctrine" of the Trinity and the Chalcedonian "doctrine" of the person of Christ. Logically, the model is put together in two stages: first, the death of Christ is declared to have been *substitutionary*; then the substitution is characterized and given a specific frame of reference by adding the word *penal*. We shall examine the two stages separately.

Stage one is to declare Christ's death *substitutionary*. What does this mean? The *Oxford English Dictionary* defines substitution as "the putting of one person or thing in the place of another." One oddity of contemporary Christian talk is that many who affirm that Jesus' death was vicarious and representative deny that it was substitutionary, for the *Dictionary* defines both words in substitutionary terms! Representation is said to mean "the fact of standing for, or in place of, some other thing or person, especially with a right or authority to act on their account; *substitution* of one thing or person for another." And vicarious is defined as

14. Cf. Vincent Taylor's remark, in *The Atonement in New Testament Teaching* (London: Epworth Press, 1940), 301f.: "The thought of *substitution* is one we have perhaps been more anxious to reject than to assess; yet the immeasurable sense of gratitude with which it is associated . . . is too great a thing to be wanting in a worthy theory of the Atonement."

"that which takes or supplies the place of another thing or person; *substituted* instead of the proper thing or person." So here, it seems, is a distinction without a difference. Substitution is, in fact, a broad idea that applies whenever one person acts to supply another's need, or to discharge his obligation, so that the other no longer has to carry the load himself. As Pannenberg says, "In social life, substitution is a universal phenomenon. . . . Even the structure of vocation, the division of labour, has substitutionary character. One who has a vocation performs this function for those whom he serves." For "every service has vicarious character by recognizing a need in the person served that apart from the service that person would have to satisfy for himself."[15] In this broad sense, nobody who wishes to say with Paul that there is a true sense in which "Christ died for us" (ὑπέρ, on our behalf, for our benefit), and "Christ redeemed us from the curse of the law, having become a curse for us" (ὑπέρ again) (Rom. 5:8; Gal. 3:13 RV), and who accepts Christ's assurance that he came "to give his life a ransom for many" (ἀντί, which means precisely "in place of," "in exchange for"[16]), should hesitate to say that Christ's death was substitutionary. Indeed, if he describes Christ's death as vicarious he is actually saying it.

It is, of course, no secret why people shy off this word. It is because they equate, and know that others equate, substitution *in* Christology with *penal* substitution. This explains the state of affairs that, writing in 1948, F. W. Camfield described as follows:

> If there is one conclusion which [has] come almost to be taken for granted in enlightened Christian quarters, it is that the idea of substitution has led theology on a wrong track; and that the word "substitution" must now be dropped from the doctrine of the Atonement as too heavily laden with misleading and even false connotations. By "liberal" or "modernist" theology the idea of substitution is of course

15. Wolfhart Pannenberg, *Jesus—God and Man*, trans. Lewis L. Wilkins and Duane A. Priebe (London: SCM, 1968), 259, 268.

16. See R. E. Davies, "Christ in Our Place—the Contribution of the Prepositions," *Tyndale Bulletin* 21 (1970), 72ff.

rejected out of hand. And even the theology which prides itself on being "positive" and "evangelical" and which seeks to maintain lines of communication with the great traditional doctrines of atonement is on the whole disposed to reject it. And this, not merely on the ground that it holds implications which are irrational and morally offensive, but even and specifically on the ground that it is unscriptural. Thus Dr. Vincent Taylor as a result of exhaustive examination of the "Idea of Atonement in the New Testament" gives it as his conclusion that the idea of substitution has no place in the New Testament writings; that in fact it is opposed to the fundamental teaching of the New Testament; that even St. Paul though he sometimes trembles on the edge of substitutionary conceptions nevertheless avoids them. It is difficult to escape the impression that Dr. Vincent Taylor's anxiety to eliminate the idea of substitution from evangelical theology has coloured his interpretation of the New Testament witness. But his conclusions provide a striking indication of the tendency at work in modern evangelical circles. It is felt that nothing has done more to bring the evangelical doctrine of the Atonement into disrepute than the idea of substitution; and therefore, something like a sigh of relief makes itself heard when it is suggested that this idea rests on a misunderstanding of the teaching of Scripture.[17]

Today, more than a quarter of a century later, the picture Camfield draws would have to be qualified by reference to the vigorous vin-

17. F. W. Camfield, "The Idea of Substitution in the Doctrine of the Atonement," *SJT* I (1948) 282f., referring to Vincent Taylor, *The Atonement in New Testament Teaching*. Taylor, while allowing that Paul "in particular, is within a hair's breadth of substitutions" (p. 288), and that "a theologian who retires to a doctrinal fortress guarded by such ordnance as Mark x. 45, Romans vi. 10f., 2 Corinthians v. 14, 21, Galatians iii. 13, and 1 Timothy ii. 5f., is more difficult to dislodge than many New Testament students imagine" (p. 289), rejects substitution as implying a redemption "wrought entirely outside of, and apart from, ourselves so that we have nothing to do but to accept its benefits" (p. 125). He describes Christ's death as a representative sacrifice, involving endurance of sin's penalty plus that archetypal expression of penitence for humanity's wrongdoing that was first conceived by McLeod Campbell and R. C. Moberly. We participate in this sacrifice, Taylor continues, by offering it on our own behalf, which we do by letting it teach us to repent. Taylor admits that from his standpoint there is "a gap in Pauline teaching. With clear eyes St Paul marks 'the one act of righteousness' in the obedience of Christ (Romans v. 18f.) and the fact that He was 'made to be sin on our behalf' (2 Corinthians v. 21), but he nowhere speaks of Him as voicing the sorrow and contrition of men in the presence of His Father" (p. 291).

dication and use of the substitution idea by such as Pannenberg and Barth;[18] nonetheless, in British theology the overall situation remains very much as Camfield describes. It would, however, clarify discussion if all who hold that Jesus by dying did something for us that we needed to do but could not, would agree that they are regarding Christ's death as substitutionary, and differing only on the nature of the action that Jesus performed in our place and also, perhaps, on the way we enter into the benefit that flows from it. Camfield himself goes on to spell out a non-penal view of substitution.

Broadly speaking, there have been three ways in which Christ's death has been explained in the church. Each reflects a particular view of the nature of God and our plight in sin and of what is needed to bring us to God in the fellowship of acceptance on his side and faith and love on ours. It is worth glancing at them to see how the idea of substitution fits in with each.

There is, first, the type of account that sees the cross as having its effect entirely on men, whether by revealing God's love to us, or by bringing home to us how much God hates our sins, or by setting us a supreme example of godliness, or by blazing a trail to God that we may now follow, or by so involving mankind in his redemptive obedience that the life of God now flows into us, or by all these modes together. It is assumed that our basic need is lack of motivation Godward and of openness to the inflow of divine life; all that is needed to set us in a right relationship with God is a change in us at these two points, and this Christ's death brings about. The forgiveness of our sins is not a separate problem; as soon as we are changed we become forgivable, and are then forgiven at once. This view has little or no room for any thought of substitution, since it goes so far in equating what Christ did *for* us with what he does *to* us.

A second type of account sees Christ's death as having its effect primarily on hostile spiritual forces external to us that are held to be imprisoning us in a captivity of which our inveterate moral twistedness is one sign and symptom. The cross is seen as the work

---

18. See Pannenberg, *op. cit.*, pp. 258–69; Barth, *Church Dogmatics* 4:1, trans. G. W. Bromiley (Edinburgh: T. and T. Clark, 1956), viif., 230ff., 550ff.

of God going forth to battle as our champion, just as David went forth as Israel's champion to fight Goliath. Through the cross these hostile forces, however conceived—whether as sin and death, Satan and his hosts, the demonic in society and its structures, the powers of God's wrath and curse, or anything else—are overcome and nullified, so that Christians are not in bondage to them, but share Christ's triumph over them. The assumption here is that man's plight is created entirely by hostile cosmic forces distinct from God; yet, seeing Jesus as our champion, exponents of this view could still properly call him our substitute, just as all the Israelites who declined Goliath's challenge in 1 Samuel 17:8–11 could properly call David their substitute. Just as a substitute who involves others in the consequences of his action, as if they had done it themselves, is their representative, so a representative discharging the obligations of those whom he represents is their substitute. What this type of account of the cross affirms (though it is not usually put in these terms) is that the conquering Christ, whose victory secured our release, was our representative substitute.

The third type of account denies nothing asserted by the other two views save their assumption that they are complete. It agrees that there is biblical support for all they say, but it goes further. It grounds man's plight as a victim of sin and Satan in the fact that, for all God's daily goodness to him, as a sinner he stands under divine judgment, and his bondage to evil is the start of his sentence, and unless God's rejection of him is turned into acceptance he is lost for ever. On this view, Christ's death had its effect first on God, who was hereby *propitiated* (or, better, who hereby propitiated himself), and only because it had this effect did it become an overthrowing of the powers of darkness and a revealing of God's seeking and saving love. The thought here is that by dying Christ offered to God what the West has called *satisfaction* for sins, satisfaction which God's own character dictated as the only means whereby his no to us could become a yes. Whether this Godward satisfaction is understood as the homage of death itself, or death as the perfecting of holy obedience, or an undergoing of the God-forsakenness of hell, which is

God's final judgment on sin, or a perfect confession of man's sins combined with entry into their bitterness by sympathetic identification, or all these things together (and nothing stops us combining them together), the shape of this view remains the same—that by undergoing the cross Jesus expiated our sins, propitiated our Maker, turned God's no to us into a yes, and so saved us. All forms of this view see Jesus as our representative substitute in fact, whether or not they call him that, but only certain versions of it represent his substitution as penal.

This analysis prompts three comments.

First, it should be noted that though the two former views regularly set themselves in antithesis to the third, the third takes up into itself all the positive assertions that they make, which raises the question whether any more is at issue here than the impropriety of treating half-truths as the whole truth, and of rejecting a more comprehensive account on the basis of speculative negations about what God's holiness requires as a basis for forgiving sins. Were it allowed that the first two views might be misunderstanding and distorting themselves in this way, the much-disputed claim that a broadly substitutionary view of the cross has always been the mainstream Christian opinion might be seen to have substance in it after all. It is a pity that books on the atonement so often take it for granted that accounts of the cross that have appeared as rivals in historical debate must be treated as intrinsically exclusive. This is always arbitrary, and sometimes quite perverse.

Second, it should be noted that our analysis was simply of views about the death of Christ, so nothing was said about his resurrection. All three types of view usually agree in affirming that the resurrection is an integral part of the gospel; that the gospel proclaims a living, vindicated Savior whose resurrection as the firstfruits of the new humanity is the basis as well as the pattern for ours is not a matter of dispute among them. It is sometimes pointed out that the second view represents the resurrection of Jesus as an organic element in his victory over the powers of death, whereas the third view does not, and hardly could, represent it as an organic element in the bearing of sin's penalty or the tasting and confessing of its vileness (however the work of Calvary is conceived); and on this basis the third view is sometimes criticized as making the resurrection unnecessary. But this criticism may be met in two ways. The first reply is that Christ's saving work has two parts: his dealing with his Father on our behalf by offering himself in substitutionary satisfaction for our sins and his dealing with us on his Father's behalf by bestowing on us through faith the forgiveness that his death secured, and it is as important to distinguish these two parts as it is to hold them together. For a demonstration that part two is now possible because part one is finished, and for the actual implementing of part two, Jesus' resurrection is indeed essential and so appears as an organic element in his work as a whole. The second reply is that these two ways of viewing the cross should in any case be synthesized, following the example of Paul in Colossians 2:13–15, as being complementary models expressing different elements in the single complex reality that is the mystery of the cross.

Third, it should be noted that not all advocates of the third type of view have been happy to use the word "substitution." This has been partly through desire to evade the Socinian criticism that in the penal realm substitution is impossible, and partly for fear that to think of Christ dying *for* us as our substitute obscures his call to us to die and rise *in* him and *with* him, for the moral transforming of us into his holy image. P. T. Forsyth, for example, is one who stresses the vicariousness of Christ's action in his passion as he endured for man's salvation God's personal anger against man's sin;[19] yet

---

19. "He turned the penalty He endured into sacrifice He offered. And the sacrifice He offered was the judgment He accepted. His passive suffering became active obedience, and obedience to a holy doom." *The Work of Christ* (London: Hodder and Stoughton, 1910), 163. In a two thousand-word "addendum" Forsyth combats the Ritschlian view, later to be espoused by C. H. Dodd, that the wrath of God is simply the "automatic recoil of His moral order upon the transgressor . . . as if there were no personal reaction of a Holy God Himself upon the sin, and no infliction of His displeasure upon the sinner" (p. 239). He argues to the position that "what Christ bore was not simply a sense of the connection between the sinner and the impersonal consequences of sin, but a sense of the sinner's relation to the personal *vis-à-vis* of an angry God. God never left him, but He did refuse Him His face. The communion was not broken, but its light was withdrawn" (p. 243).

he rejects "substitution" in favor of "representation" and replaces "substitutionary expiation" (which, as these words are commonly understood, leaves us too little committed) by "solidary reparation," "solidary confession and praise," because he wants to stress that we enter into salvation only as we identify with Christ's death to sin and are re-created as the new humanity in him.[20] But, admirable as is Forsyth's wish to stress what is in Romans 6:1–11, avoiding the word *substitution* can only have the effect of obscuring what is in Romans 3:21–28, where Paul describes Christ as "a propitiation[21] by his blood" (v. 25 ESV) in virtue of which God bestows "the free gift of righteousness" (5:17 ESV) upon believing sinners and so "justifies the ungodly" (4:5 ESV). As James Denney said, "If Christ died the death in which sin had involved us—if in His death He took the responsibility of our sins on Himself—no word is equal to this which falls short of what is meant by calling Him our substitute."[22]

20. Op. cit., 164, 182, 223, 225f. "Substitution does not take account of the moral results (of the cross) on the soul," 182n.

21. "Propitiation" (which means quenching God's wrath against sinners) is replaced by "expiation" (which means removing sins from God's sight) in RSV and other modern versions. The idea of propitiation includes that of expiation as its means; thus the effect of this change is not to bring in a sacrificial motif that was previously absent, but to cut out a reference to quenching God's anger that was previously thought to be present. The case for "expiation" was put forward by C. H. Dodd in 1935 and at first gained wide support, but a generation of debate has shown that "the linguistic evidence seems to favour 'propitiation.'" Matthew Black, *Romans*, New Century Bible (London: Oliphants, 1973), 68. See the full coverage of literature cited by Black, and also David Hill, *Greek Words and Hebrew Meanings* (Cambridge: Cambridge University Press, 1967), 23–48.

22. James Denney, *The Death of Christ*, 2nd ed., including *The Atonement and the Modern Mind* (London: Hodder and Stoughton, 1911), 73. Denney's summary of the meaning of Rom. 3:25f. is worth quoting:

It is Christ set forth in His blood who is a propitiation; that is, it is Christ who died. In dying, as St. Paul conceived it, He made our sin His own; He took it on Himself as the reality which it is in God's sight and to God's law: He became sin, became a curse for us. It is this which gives His death a propitiatory character and power; in other words, which makes it possible for God to be at once righteous and a God who accepts as righteous those who believe in Jesus. . . . I do not know any word which conveys the truth of this if 'vicarious' or 'substitutionary' does not, nor do I know any interpretation of Christ's death which enables us to regard it as a demonstration of love to sinners, if this vicarious or substitutionary character is denied (p. 126).

Denney's point in the last sentence is that Christ's death only reveals God's love if it accomplished something that we needed, that we could not do for ourselves, and that Christ could not do without dying.

The correct reply to Forsyth would seem to be that before Christ's death can be representative, in Forsyth's sense of setting a pattern of "confession and praise" to be reproduced in our own self-denial and cross-bearing, it has to be substitutionary in Denney's sense of absorbing God's wrath against our sins; otherwise, our "confession and praise" in solidarity with Christ becomes itself a ploy for averting that wrath—in other words, a meritorious work, aimed at securing pardon, assuming that in Christ we save ourselves.

What Denney said about this in 1903 was in fact an answer by anticipation to Forsyth's formula of 1910. A reviewer of *The Death of Christ* had argued that "if we place ourselves at Paul's point of view, we shall see that to the eye of God the death of Christ presents itself less as an act which Christ does for the race than as an act which the race does in Christ." In *The Atonement and the Modern Mind* Denney quoted these words and commented on them thus:

> In plain English, Paul teaches less that Christ died for the ungodly, than that the ungodly in Christ died for themselves. This brings out the logic of what representative means when representative is opposed to substitute.[23] The representative is ours, we are in Him, and we are supposed to get over all the moral difficulties raised by the idea of substitution just because He is ours, and because we are one with Him. But the fundamental fact of the situation is that, to begin with, Christ is *not* ours, and we are *not* one with Him. . . . We are 'without Christ' (χωρὶς Χριστοῦ). . . . A representative not produced by us, but given to us—not chosen by us, but the elect of God—is not a representative at all in the first instance, but a substitute.[24]

23. It should be noted that in addition to the rather specialized usage that Denney has in view, whereby one's "representative" is the one whose behavior is taken as the model for one's own, "representative" may (and usually does) signify simply this: that one's status is such that one involves others, for good or ill, in the consequences of what one does. In this sense, families are represented by fathers; nations by kings, presidents, and government ministers; and humanity by Adam and Christ; and it was as our representative in this sense that Jesus became our substitute.

24. James Denney, *The Death of Christ*, 304; cf. 307, "Union with Christ" (i.e., personal, moral union, by faith) ". . . is not a presupposition of Christ's work, it is its fruit."

So the true position, on the type of view we are exploring, may be put thus: We identify with Christ against the practice of sin because we have already identified him as the one who took our place under sentence for sin. We enter upon the life of repentance because we have learned that he first endured for us the death of reparation. The Christ into whom we now accept incorporation is the Christ who previously on the cross became our propitiation—not, therefore, one in whom we achieve our reconciliation with God, but one through whom we receive it as a free gift based on a finished work (cf. Rom. 5:10); and we love him, because he first loved us and gave himself for us. So substitution, in this view, really is the basic category; the thought of Christ as our representative, however construed in detail, cannot be made to mean what substitution means, and our solidarity with Christ in "confession and praise," so far from being a concept alternative to that of substitution, is actually a response that presupposes it.

Penal Substitution

Now we move to the second stage in our model-building and bring in the word "penal" to characterize the substitution we have in view. To add this "qualifier," as Ramsey would call it, is to anchor the model of substitution (not exclusively, but regulatively) within the world of moral law, guilty conscience, and retributive justice. Thus is forged a conceptual instrument for conveying the thought that God remits our sins and accepts our persons into favor not because of any amends we have attempted, but because the penalty that was our due was diverted on to Christ. The notion which the phrase "penal substitution" expresses is that Jesus Christ our Lord, moved by a love that was determined to do everything necessary to save us, endured and exhausted the destructive divine judgment for which we were otherwise inescapably destined, and so won us forgiveness, adoption, and glory. To affirm penal substitution is to say that believers are in debt to Christ specifically for this, and that this is the mainspring of all their joy, peace, and praise both now and for eternity.

The general thought is clear enough, but for our present purpose we need a fuller analysis of its meaning, and here a methodological choice must be made. Should we appeal to particular existing accounts of penal substitution, or construct a composite of our own? At the risk of seeming idiosyncratic (which is, I suppose, the gentleman's way of saying unsound) I plump for the latter course, for the following main reasons.

First, there is no denying that penal substitution sometimes has been, and still sometimes is, asserted in ways that merit the favorite adjective of its critics—"crude." As one would expect of that which for more than four centuries has been the mainspring of evangelical piety—"popular piety," as Roman Catholics would call it—ways of presenting it have grown up that are devotionally evocative without always being theologically rigorous. Moreover, the more theological expositions of it since Socinus have tended to be one-track-minded; constricted in interest by the preoccupations of controversy, and absorbed in the task of proclaiming the one vital truth about the cross that others disregarded or denied, "upholders of the penal theory have sometimes so stressed the thought that Christ bore our penalty that they have found room for nothing else. Rarely have they in theory denied the value of other theories, but sometimes they have in practice ignored them."[25] Also, as we have seen, much of the more formative and influential discussing of penal substitution was done in the seventeenth century, at a time when Protestant exegesis of Scripture was colored by an uncriticized and indeed unrecognized natural theology of law, and this has left its mark on many later statements. All this being so, it might be hard to find an account of penal substitution that could safely be taken as standard or as fully representative, and it will certainly be more straightforward if I venture an analysis of my own.

Second, I have already hinted that I think it important for the theory of penal substitution to be evaluated as a model setting forth the meaning of the atonement rather than its mechanics. One re-

25. Leon Morris, *The Cross in the New Testament* (Exeter: Paternoster, 1965), 401.

sult of the work of rationalistic Protestant theologians over three centuries, from the Socinians to the Hegelians, was to nourish the now common assumption that the logical function of a "theory" in theology is to resolve "how" problems within an established frame of thought about God and man. In other words, theological theories are like detectives' theories in whodunits; they are hypotheses relating puzzling facts together in such a way that all puzzlement is dispelled (for the convention of "mystery stories" is that by the last page no mystery should be felt to remain). Now we have seen that, for discernible historical reasons, penal substitution has sometimes been explicated as a theory of this kind, telling us how divine love and justice could be, and were, "reconciled" (whatever that means); but a doubt remains as to whether this way of understanding the theme is biblically right. Is the harmonization of God's attributes any part of the information, or is it even the kind of information, that the inspired writers are concerned to give?

Gustaf Aulén characterized the *Christus victor* motif (he would not call it a theory) as a dramatic idea of the atonement rather than a rationale of its mechanics, and contrasted it in this respect with the "Latin" view, of which penal substitution is one form;[26] but should not penal substitution equally be understood as a dramatic idea, declaring the fact of the atonement kerygmatically, i.e., as gospel (good news), just as Aulén's conquest motif is concerned to do? I believe it should. Surely the primary issue with which penal substitution is concerned is neither the morality nor the rationality of God's ways, but the remission of my sins; and the primary function of the concept is to correlate my knowledge of being guilty before God with my knowledge that, on the one hand, no question of my ever being judged for my sins can now arise, and, on the other hand, that the risen Christ whom I am called to accept as Lord is none other than Jesus, who secured my immunity from judgment by bearing on the cross the penalty that was my due. The effect of this correlation is not in any sense to "solve" or dissipate the mystery of the work of God (it is not that sort of mystery!); the effect is simply

26. *Christus Victor*, 175.

to define that work with precision, and thus to evoke faith, hope, praise, and responsive love to Jesus Christ. So, at least, I think, and therefore I wish my presentation of penal substitution to highlight its character as a kerygmatic model; and so I think it best to offer my own analytical definition, which will aim to be both descriptive of what all who have held this view had had in common, and also prescriptive of how the term should be understood in any future discussion.

Third, if the present examination of penal substitution is to be worthwhile, it must present this view in its best light, and I think an eclectic exposition will bring us closest to this goal. The typical modern criticism of older expositions of our theme is that, over and above their being less than fully moral (Socinus's criticism), they are less than fully personal. Thus, for instance, C. W. H. Lampe rejects penal substitution because it assumes that "God inflicts retributive punishment," and "retribution is impersonal; it considers offences in the abstract. . . . We ought not to ascribe purely retributive justice to God. . . . The Father of mankind does not deal with his children on the basis of deterrence and retribution. . . . To hang the criminal is to admit defeat at the level of love. . . . It is high time to discard the vestiges of a theory of Atonement that was geared to a conception of punishment which found nothing shocking in the idea that God should crucify sinners or the substitute who took their place. It is time, too, to stop the mouth of the blasphemer who calls it 'sentimentality' to reject the idea of a God of retribution."[27] Lampe's violent language shows the strength of his conviction that retribution belongs to a sub-personal, nonloving order of relationships, and that penal substitution dishonors the cross by anchoring it here.

James Denney's sense of the contrast between personal relations, which are moral, and legal relations, which tend to be impersonal, external, and arbitrary, once drew from him an outburst that in isolation might seem parallel to Lampe's:

27. G. W. H. Lampe, "The Atonement: Law and Love," in *Soundings*, ed. A. R. Vidler (Cambridge: Cambridge University Press, 1962), 187ff.

> Few things have astonished me more than to be charged with teaching a "forensic" or "legal" or "judicial" doctrine of Atonement. . . . There is nothing that I should wish to reprobate more whole-heartedly than the conception which is expressed by these words. To say that the relations of God and man are forensic is to say that they are regulated by statute—that sin is a breach of statute—that the sinner is a criminal—and that God adjudicates on him by interpreting the statute in its application to his case. Everybody knows that this is a travesty of the truth.[28]

It is noticeable that Denney, the champion of the substitutionary idea, never calls Christ's substitution "penal"; in his situation, the avoidance must have been deliberate. Yet Denney affirmed these four truths: first, that "the relations of God and man . . . are personal, but . . . determined by (moral) law"; second, "that there is in the nature of things a reaction against sin which when it has had its perfect work is fatal, that this reaction is the divine punishment of sin, and that its finally fatal character is what is meant by Scripture when it says that the wages of sin is death"; third, that "the inevitable reactions of the divine order against evil . . . are the sin itself coming back in another form and finding out the sinner. They are nothing if not retributive"; and, fourth, "that while the agony and the Passion were not penal in the sense of coming upon Jesus through a bad conscience, or making Him the personal object of divine wrath, they were penal in the sense that in that dark hour He had to realise to the full the divine reaction against sin in the race . . . and that without doing so He could not have been the Redeemer of that race from sin."[29] It seems to me

---

28. James Denney, from *The Atonement and the Modern Mind*, 271f. Denney's last sentence overstates; as J. S. Whale says, "The Christian religion has thought of Christ not only as Victor and as Victim, but also as 'Criminal,'" and all three models (Whale calls them metaphors) have biblical justification (*Victor and Victim*, Cambridge: Cambridge University Press, 1960), 70.

29. James Denney, *The Christian Doctrine of Reconciliation* (London: Hodder and Stoughton, 1917), 187, 214, 208, 273. On pp. 262f. and elsewhere Denney rejects as unintelligible all notions of a quantitative equivalence between Christ's actual sufferings and those which sinners would have to endure under ultimate judgment; "to realize to the full the divine reaction against sin in the race," whatever it meant, did not mean that.

that these affirmations point straight to a way of formulating the penal substitution model that is both moral and personal enough to evade all Lampe's strictures and also inclusive of all that the concept means to those who embrace it. But the formulation itself will have to be my own.

So I shall now attempt my analysis of penal substitution as a model of the atonement, under five heads: substitution and retribution; substitution and solidarity; substitution and mystery; substitution and salvation; substitution and divine love. Others who espouse this model must judge whether I analyze it accurately or not.

1) Substitution and Retribution

Penal substitution, as an idea, presupposes a penalty (*poena*) due to us from God the Judge for wrong done and failure to meet his claims. The *locus classicus* on this is Romans 1:18–3:20, but the thought is everywhere in the New Testament. The judicial context is a moral context too; whereas human judicial systems are not always rooted in moral reality, the Bible treats the worlds of moral reality and of divine judgment as coinciding. Divine judgment means that retribution is entailed by our past upon our present and future existence, and God himself is in charge of this process, ensuring that the objective wrongness and guiltiness of what we have been is always "there" to touch and wither what we are and shall be. In the words of Emil Brunner, "Guilt means that our past—that which can never be made good—always constitutes one element in our present situation."[30]

When Lady Macbeth, walking and talking in her sleep, sees blood on her hand, and cannot clean or sweeten it, she witnesses to the order of retribution as all writers of tragedy and surely all reflective men—certainly, those who believe in penal substitution—have come to know it: wrongdoing may be forgotten for a time, as David forgot his sin over Bathsheba and Uriah, but sooner or later it comes back to mind, as David's sin did under Nathan's ministry; at once our at-

---

30. Emil Brunner, *The Mediator*, trans. O. Wyon (London: Lutterworth Press, 1934), 443.

tention is absorbed, our peace and pleasure are gone, and something tells us that we ought to suffer for what we have done. When joined with inklings of God's displeasure, this sense of things is the start of hell. Now it is into this context of awareness that the model of penal substitution is introduced to focus for us four insights about our situation.

Insight one concerns God: it is that the retributive principle has his sanction, and indeed expresses the holiness, justice, and goodness reflected in his law, and that death, spiritual as well as physical, the loss of the life of God as well as that of the body, is the rightful sentence that he has announced against us and now prepares to inflict.

Insight two concerns ourselves: it is that, standing thus under sentence, we are helpless either to undo the past or to shake off sin in the present, and thus have no way of averting what threatens.

Insight three concerns Jesus Christ: it is that he, the God-man of John 1:1–18 and Hebrews 1–2, took our place under judgment and received in his own personal experience all the dimensions of the death that was our sentence, whatever these were, so laying the foundation for our pardon and immunity.

> We may not know, we cannot tell
> What pains he had to bear;
> But we believe it was for us
> He hung and suffered there.

Insight four concerns faith: it is that faith is a matter first and foremost of looking outside and away from oneself to Christ and his cross as the sole ground of present forgiveness and future hope. Faith sees that God's demands remain what they were, and that God's law of retribution, which our conscience declares to be right, has not ceased to operate in his world, nor ever will; but that in our case the law has operated already, so that all our sins, past, present, and even future, have been covered by Calvary. So our conscience is pacified by the knowledge that our sins have already been judged and punished, however strange the statement may sound, in the person and death of another. Bunyan's pilgrim before the cross loses his burden, and Toplady can assure himself:

> If thou my pardon hast secured,
> And freely in my room endured
> The whole of wrath divine,
> Payment God cannot twice demand,
> First from my bleeding surety's hand
> And then again from mine.

Reasoning thus, faith grasps the reality of God's free gift of righteousness, i.e., the "rightness" with God that the righteous enjoy (cf. Rom. 5:16f.), and with it the justified man's obligation to live henceforth "unto" the one who for his sake died and rose again (cf. 2 Cor. 5:14).

This analysis, if correct, shows what job the word "penal" does in our model. It is there, not to prompt theoretical puzzlement about the transferring of guilt, but to articulate the insight of believers who, as they look at Calvary in the light of the New Testament, are constrained to say, "Jesus was bearing the judgment I deserved (and deserve), the penalty for my sins, the punishment due to me" —"he loved me, and gave himself for me" (Gal. 2:20). How it was possible for him to bear their penalty they do not claim to know, any more than they know how it was possible for him to be made man; but that he bore it is the certainty on which all their hopes rest.

2) *Substitution and Solidarity*

Anticipating the rationalistic criticism that guilt is not transferable and the substitution described, if real, would be immoral, our model now invokes Paul's description of the Lord Jesus Christ as the second man and last Adam, who involved us in his sin bearing as truly as Adam involved us in his sinning (cf. 1 Cor. 15:45ff.; Rom. 5:12 ff.). Penal substitution was seen by Luther, the pioneer in stating it, and by those who came after, as grounded in this ontological solidarity, and as being one "moment" in the larger mystery of what Luther called "a wonderful exchange"[31] and Dr. Morna Hooker designates "interchange in Christ."[32] In this mystery there are four "moments" to be distinguished. The first is the incarnation when the Son of God came into the human situation, "born of a woman, born under the law, that he might redeem them which were under the law" (Gal. 4:4f. RV). The second "moment" was the cross, where Jesus, as Luther and Calvin put it, carried our identity[33] and effectively involved us

31. Two quotations give Luther's viewpoint here. The first is from his exposition of Psalm 21 (22):

> This is that mystery which is rich in divine grace to sinners: wherein by *a wonderful exchange* our sins are no longer ours but Christ's: and the righteousness of Christ not Christ's but ours. He has emptied himself of his righteousness that he might clothe us with it, and fill us with it: and he has taken our evils upon himself that he might deliver us from them . . . in the same manner as he grieved and suffered in our sins, and was confounded, in the same manner we rejoice and glory in his righteousness. *Werke* (Weimar, 1883), 5:608.

The second is from a pastoral letter to George Spenlein: "Learn Christ and him crucified. Learn to pray to him and, despairing of yourself, say: 'Thou, Lord Jesus, art my righteousness, but I am thy sin. Thou hast taken upon thyself what is mine and hast given to me what is thine. Thou hast taken upon thyself what thou wast not and hast given to me what I was not.'" *Letters of Spiritual Counsel*, ed. Theodore G. Tappert, Library of Christian Classics (London: SCM Press, 1955), 110.

32. Article in *JTS* 22 (1971) 349–61.

33. Luther puts this dramatically and exuberantly, as was always his way:

> All the prophets did foresee in spirit, that Christ should become the greatest transgressor, murderer, adulterer, thief, rebel, blasphemer, etc., that ever was . . . for he being made a sacrifice, for the sins of the whole world, is not now an innocent person and without sins. . . . Our most merciful Father . . . sent his only Son into the world and laid upon him the sins of all men, saying: Be thou Peter that denier; Paul that persecutor, blasphemer and cruel oppressor; David that adulterer; that sinner which did eat the apple in Paradise; that thief which hanged upon the cross; and, briefly, be thou the person which hath committed the sins of all men; see therefore that thou pay and satisfy for them. Here now cometh the law and saith: I find him a sinner . . . therefore let him die upon the cross. *Galatians*, ed. Philip S. Watson (London: James Clarke, 1953), 269–71; on Gal. 3:13.

Aulén (*Christus Victor*, chap. 6) rightly stresses the dynamism of divine victory in Luther's account of the cross and resurrection, but wrongly ignores the penal substitution in terms of which Christ's victorious work is basically defined. The essence of Christ's victory, according to Luther, is that on the cross as our substitute he effectively purged our sins, so freeing us from Satin's power by overcoming God's curse; if Luther's whole treatment of Gal. 3:13 (pp. 268–82) is read, this becomes very plain. The necessary supplement, and indeed correction, of the impression Aulén leaves is provided by Pannenberg's statement (op. cit., 279): "Luther was probably the first since Paul and his school to have seen with full clarity that Jesus' death in its genuine sense is to be understood as vicarious

all in his dying; as Paul says, "One died for all, therefore all died" (2 Cor. 5:14 RV). Nor is this sharing in Christ's death a legal fiction, a form of words to which no reality corresponds; it is part of the objective fact of Christ, the mystery that is "there" whether we grasp it or not. So now Christ's substitution for us, which is exclusive in the sense of making the work of atonement wholly his and allowing us no share in performing it, is seen to be from another standpoint inclusive of us, inasmuch as ontologically and objectively, in a manner transcending bounds of space and time, Christ has taken us with him into his death and through his death into his resurrection.

Thus knowledge of Christ's death for us as our sin-bearing substitute requires us to see ourselves as dead, risen, and alive for evermore in him. We who believe have died—painlessly and invisibly, we might say—in solidarity with him because he died, painfully and publicly, in substitution for us. His death for us brought remission of sins committed "in" Adam, so that "in" him we might enjoy God's acceptance; our death "in" him brings release from the existence we knew "in" Adam, so that "in" him we are raised to new life and become new creatures (cf. Rom. 5–6; 2 Cor. 5:17, 21; Col. 2:6–3:4). The third "moment" in this interchange comes when, through faith and God's gift of the Spirit, we become "the righteousness of God" and "rich"—that is, justified from sin and accepted as heirs of God in and with Christ—by virtue of him who became "poor"' for us in the incarnation and was "made sin" for us by penal substitution on the cross (cf. 2 Cor. 5:21; 8:9). And the fourth "moment" will be when this same Jesus Christ, who was exalted to glory after being humbled to death for us, reappears to "fashion anew the body of

---

penal suffering." Calvin makes the same point in his more precise way, commenting on Jesus' trial before Pilate. "When he was arraigned before a judgment-seat, accused and put under pressure by testimony, and sentenced to death by the words of a judge, we know by these records that he played the part (*personam sustinuit*) of a guilty wrongdoer . . . we see the role of sinner and criminal represented in Christ, yet from his shining innocence it becomes obvious that he was burdened with the misdoing of others rather than his own. . . . This is our acquittal, that the guilt which exposed us to punishment was transferred to the head of God's Son. . . . At every point he substituted himself in our place (*in vicem nostram ubique se supposuerit*) to pay the price of our redemption" (*Inst.* 2:xvi. 5, 7). It is inexplicable that Pannenberg (loc. cit.) should say that Calvin retreated from Luther's insight into penal substitution.

our humiliation, that it may be conformed to the body of his glory" (cf. Phil. 2:5–11; 3:21).

Sometimes it is urged that in relation to this comprehensive mystery of solidarity and interchange, viewed as a whole, Christ the "pioneer" (ἀρχηαγόσ: Heb. 2:10; 12:2) is best designated the "representative" and "first-fruits" of the new humanity, rather than be called our substitute.[34] Inasmuch as the interchange theme centers upon our renewal in Christ's image, this point may be readily accepted, provided it is also seen that in relation to the particular mystery of sin bearing, which is at the heart of the interchange, Christ as victim of the penal process has to be called our substitute, since the purpose and effect of his suffering was precisely to ensure that no such suffering—no Godforsakenness, no dereliction—should remain for us. In the light of earlier discussion[35] we are already entitled to dismiss the proposal to call Christ's death representative rather than substitutionary as both confusing and confused, since it suggests, first, that we chose Christ to act for us; second, that the death we die in him is of the same order as the death he died for us; and third, that by dying in Christ we atone for our sins—all of which are false. Here now is a further reason for rejecting the proposal—namely, that it misses or muffs the point that what Christ bore on the cross was the God-forsakenness of penal judgment, which we shall never have to bear because he accepted it in our place. The appropriate formulation is that on the cross Jesus' representative relation to us, as the last Adam whose image we are to bear, took the form of substituting for us under judgment as the suffering servant of God on whom the Lord "laid the iniquity of us all."[36] The two ideas,

34. For "representative," cf. M. D. Hooker, art. cit., 358, and G. W. H. Lampe, *Reconciliation in Christ* (London: Longmans, 1956), chap. 3; for "first-fruits," cf. D. E. H. Whiteley, *The Theology of St. Paul* (Oxford: Blackwell, 1964), 132ff. The preferred usage of these authors seems to reflect both awareness of solidarity between Christ and us and also failure to recognize that what forgiveness rests on is Christ's vicarious sin bearing, as distinct from the new obedience to which, in Dr. Hooker's phrase, we are "lifted" by Christ's action.

35. Cf. pp. 74–77 above.

36. Isa. 53:6. J. S. Whale observes that this Servant-song "makes twelve distinct and explicit statements that the Servant suffers the *penalty* of other men's sins: not only vicarious suffering but penal substitution is the plain meaning of its fourth, fifth and sixth verses. These may not be precise statements of Western forensic ideas"—and our earlier

representation and substitution, are complementary, not alternatives, and both are needed here.

3) *Substitution and Mystery*

It will by now be clear that those who affirm penal substitution offer this model not as an explanatory analysis of what lay "behind" Christ's atoning death in the way that the laws of heat provide an explanatory analysis of what lies "behind" the boiling of a kettle, but rather as a pointer directing attention to various fundamental features of the mystery—that is, according to our earlier definition, the transcendent and not-wholly-comprehensible divine reality—of Christ's atoning death itself, as the New Testament writers declare it. Most prominent among these features are the mysterious divine love that was its source, and of which it is the measure (cf. Rom. 5:8; 1 John 4:8–10; John 15:13); the mysterious necessity for it, evident from Paul's witness in Romans 8:32 that God did not spare his Son but gave him up to death for us, which shows that, he being he, he could not have saved us at any less cost to himself; the mysterious solidarity in virtue of which Christ could be "made sin" by the imputing to him of our answerability and could die for our sins in our place, and we could be "made righteous" before God through faith by the virtue of his obedience (cf. Rom. 5:17–19; 2 Cor. 5:21); and the mysterious mode of union whereby, without any diminution of our individuality as persons, or his, Christ and we are "in" each other in such a sense that already we have passed with him through death into risen life. Recognition of these mysteries causes no embarrassment, nor need it; since the cross is undeniably central in the New Testament witness to God's work, it was only to be expected

---

argument prompts the comment, a good job too!—"but they are clearly connected with penalty, inflicted through various forms of punishment that the Servant endured on other men's behalf and in their stead, because the Lord so ordained. This legal or law-court metaphor of atonement may be stated positively or negatively: either as penalty that the Redeemer takes upon himself, or as acquittal that sets the prisoner free. But in either way of stating it the connotation is substitutionary:

> In my place condemned he stood;
> Sealed my pardon with his blood" (op. cit., 69f.)

that more dimensions of mystery would be found clustered here than anywhere. (Indeed, there are more than we listed; for a full statement, the tri-unity of the loving God, the incarnation itself, and God's predestining the free acts of his enemies, would also have to come in.) To the question, what does the cross mean in God's plan for man's good, a biblical answer is ready to hand, but when we ask how these things can be we find ourselves facing mystery at every point.

Rationalistic criticism since Socinus has persistently called in question both the solidarity on which substitution is based and the need for penal satisfaction as a basis for forgiveness. This, however, is "naturalistic" criticism, which assumes that what man could not do or would not require God will not do or require either. Such criticism is profoundly perverse, for it shrinks God the Creator into the image of man the creature and loses sight of the paradoxical quality of the gospel of which the New Testament is so clearly aware. (When man justifies the wicked, it is a miscarriage of justice that God hates, but when God justifies the ungodly it is a miracle of grace for us to adore [Prov. 17:15; Rom. 4:5].) The way to stand against naturalistic theology is to keep in view its reductionist method that makes man the standard for God; to stress that according to Scripture the Creator and his work are of necessity mysterious to us, even as revealed (to make this point is the proper logical task of the word "supernatural" in theology); and to remember that what is above reason is not necessarily *against* it. As regards the atonement, the appropriate response to the Socinian critique starts by laying down that all our understanding of the cross comes from attending to the biblical witnesses and learning to hear and echo what they say about it; speculative rationalism breeds only misunderstanding, nothing more.

4) Substitution and Salvation

So far our analysis has, I think, expressed the beliefs of all who would say that penal substitution is the key to understanding the cross. But now comes a point of uncertainty and division. That Christ's penal substitution for us under divine judgment is the sole meritorious ground on which our relationship with God is restored, and is in this sense decisive for our salvation, is a Reformation point against Rome[37] to which all conservative Protestants hold. But in ordinary everyday contexts substitution is a definite and precise relationship whereby the specific obligations of one or more persons are taken over and discharged by someone else (as on the memorable occasion when I had to cry off a meeting at two days' notice due to an air strike and found afterwards that Billy Graham had consented to speak as my substitute). Should we not then think of Christ's substitution for us on the cross as a definite, one-to-one relationship between him and each individual sinner? This seems scriptural, for Paul says, "He loved *me* and gave himself for *me*" (Gal. 2:20 ESV). But if Christ specifically took and discharged my penal obligation as a sinner, does it not follow that the cross was decisive for my salvation not only as its sole meritorious ground, but also as guaranteeing that I should be brought to faith, and through faith to eternal life? For is not the faith that receives salvation part of God's gift of salvation, according to what is affirmed in Philippians 1:29 and John 6:44f. and implied in what Paul says of *God calling* and John of *new birth*?[38] And if Christ by his death on my behalf secured reconciliation and righteousness as gifts for me to receive (Rom. 5:11, 17), did not this make it certain that the faith that receives these gifts would also be given me, as a direct consequence of Christ's dying for me? Once this is granted, however, we are shut up to a choice between universalism and some form of the view that Christ died to save only a part of the human race. But if we reject these options, what have we left? The only coherent alternative is to suppose that though God purposed to save every man through the cross, some thwart his purpose by persistent unbelief. This can only be said if one is ready to maintain that God, after all, does no more than make faith possible, and then

---

37. Cf. Anglican Article XI: "We are accounted righteous before God, only for the merit of our Lord and Saviour Jesus Christ by Faith, and not for our own works or deservings."

38. Cf. John 1:12f., 3:3–15; Rom. 1:6, 7; 8:28, 30; 9:11, 24; 1 Cor. 1:9, 24, 26; Gal. 1:15; Eph. 4:4; 1 Thess. 2:12; 5:24; 2 Thess. 2:14; 2 Tim. 1:9; 1 John 5:1.

in some sense that is decisive for him as well as us leaves it to us to make faith actual.

Moreover, any who take this position must redefine substitution in imprecise terms, if indeed they do not drop the term altogether, for they are committing themselves to deny that Christ's vicarious sacrifice ensures anyone's salvation. Also, they have to give up Toplady's position—"Payment God cannot twice demand, First from my bleeding surety's hand, And then again from mine"—for it is of the essence of their view that some whose sins Christ bore, with saving intent, will ultimately pay the penalty for those same sins in their own persons. So it seems that if we are going to affirm penal substitution for all without exception, we must either infer universal salvation or else, to evade this inference, deny the saving efficacy of the substitution for anyone; and if we are going to affirm penal substitution as an effective saving act of God, we must either infer universal salvation or else, to evade this inference, restrict the scope of the substitution, making it a substitution for some, not all.[39]

All this is familiar ground to students of the Arminian controversy of the first half of the seventeenth century and of the conservative Reformed tradition since that time;[40] only the presentation is novel, since I have ventured to point up the problem as one of defining Christ's substitution, taking this as the key word for the view we are exploring. In modern usage that indeed is what it is, but only during the past century has it become so; prior to that, all conservative Protestants, at least in the English-speaking world, preferred

39. "Unless we believe in the final restoration of all mankind, we cannot have an unlimited atonement. On the premise that some perish eternally we are shut up to one of two alternatives—a limited efficacy or a limited extent; there is no such thing as an unlimited atonement." John Murray, *The Atonement* (Philadelphia: Presbyterian and Reformed, 1962), 27.

40. Cf. W. Cunningham, *Historical Theology* (London: Banner of Truth, 1960), 2:337–70; C. Hodge, *Systematic Theology* (London: Nelson, 1974), 2:544–62. The classical anti-Arminian polemic on the atonement remains John Owen's *The Death of Death in the Death of Christ* (1648: *Works*, ed. W. Goold [London: Banner of Truth, 1968]), 10:139ff., on the argumentation of which J. McLeod Campbell commented: "As addressed to those who agreed with him as to the nature of the atonement, while differing with him as to the extent of its reference, this seems unanswerable." *The Nature of the Atonement*, 4th ed. (London: Macmillan, 1873), 51.

"satisfaction" as the label and key word for their doctrine of the cross.[41]

As I pointed it up, the matter in debate might seem purely verbal, but there is more to it than that. The question is whether the thought that substitution entails salvation does or does not belong to the convictional "weave" of Scripture, to which "penal substitution" as a theological model must conform. There seems little doubt as to the answer. Though the New Testament writers do not discuss the question in anything like this form, nor is their language about the cross always as guarded as language has to be once debate on the problem has begun, they do in fact constantly take for granted that the death of Christ is the act of God that has made certain the salvation of those who are saved. The use made of the categories of ransom, redemption, reconciliation, sacrifice, and victory; the many declarations of God's purpose that Christ through the cross should save those given him, the church, his sheep and friends, God's people; the many statements viewing Christ's heavenly intercession and work *in* men as the outflow of what he did *for* them by his death; and the uniform view of faith as a means, not of meriting, but of receiving—all these features point unambiguously in one direction.

Twice in Romans Paul makes explicit his conviction that Christ's having died "for" (ὑπέρ) us—that is, us who now believe—guarantees final blessedness. In 5:8f. he says: "While we were yet sinners, Christ died for us. Much more then, being now justified by his blood, shall we be saved from the wrath through him" (KJV). In 8:32 he asks: "He that spared not his own Son, but delivered him up for us all, how shall he not also with him freely give us all things?" (KJV).

---

41. Thus, in *The Atonement* (1868) A. A. Hodge, while speaking freely, as his Reformed predecessors did, of Christ as our substitute in a strict sense under God's penal law, complained that in theology the word *substitution* had no fixed meaning, and organized his exposition round the idea of "satisfaction," which he claimed was more precise than "atonement" and was the word "habitually used by all the Reformers in all the creeds and great classical theological writings of the seventeenth century, both Lutheran and Reformed" (31ff., 37f.). By contrast the I.V. F.-U.C.C.F. Basis (1922) speaks of "redemption from the guilt, penalty and power of sin *only* through the sacrificial death (as our Representative and Substitute) of Jesus Christ," not mentioning satisfaction at all, and L. Berkhof's textbook presents Hodge's view, which it accepts entirely, as "the penal substitutionary or satisfaction doctrine" (*Systematic Theology*, 373).

Moreover, Paul and John explicitly depict God's saving work as a unity in which Christ's death fulfills a purpose of election and leads on to what the Puritans called "application of redemption"—God "calling" and "drawing" unbelievers to himself, justifying them from their sins, and giving them life as they believe, and finally glorifying them with Christ in his own presence.[42] To be sure, Paul and John insist, as all the New Testament does, that God in the gospel promises life and salvation to *everyone* who believes and calls on Christ (cf. John 3:16; Rom. 10:13); this, indeed, is to them the primary truth, and when the plan of salvation appears in their writings (in John's case, on the lips of our Lord), its logical role is to account for, and give hope of, the phenomenon of sinners responding to God's promise. Thus, through the knowledge that God is resolved to evoke the response he commands, Christians are assured of being kept safe, and evangelists of not laboring in vain. It may be added: is there any good reason for finding difficulty with the notion that the cross *both* justifies the "free offer" of Christ to all men *and also* guarantees the believing, the accepting, and the glorifying of those who respond, when this was precisely what Paul and John affirmed?

At all events, if the use historically made of the penal substitution model is examined, there is no doubt, despite occasional contusions of thought, that part of the intention is to celebrate the decisiveness of the cross as in every sense the procuring cause of salvation.

5) Substitution and Divine Love

The penal substitution model has been criticized for depicting a kind Son placating a fierce Father in order to make him love man, which he did not do before. The criticism is, however, inept, for penal substitution is a Trinitarian model, for which the motivational unity of Father and Son is axiomatic. The New Testament presents God's gift of his Son to die as the supreme expression of his love to men. "God so loved the world that he gave his only-begotten Son" (John 3:16 KJV). "God is love, . . . Herein is love, not that we loved

---

42. Cf. John 6:37–45; 10:11–16, 27–29; 17:6–26; Rom. 8:28–39; Eph. 1:3–14; 5:25–27.

God, but that he loved us, and sent his Son to be the propitiation for our sins" (1 John 4:8–10 KJV). "God shows his love for us in that while we were still sinners Christ died for us" (Rom. 5:8 ESV). Similarly, the New Testament presents the Son's voluntary acceptance of death as the supreme expression of his love to men. "He loved me, and gave himself for me" (Gal. 2:20). "Greater love has no man than this, that a man lay down his life for his friends. You are my friends . . ." (John 15:13f. RSV). And the two loves, the love of Father and Son, are one: a point that the penal substitution model, as used, firmly grasps.

Furthermore, if the true measure of love is how low it stoops to help, and how much in its humility it is ready to do and bear, then it may fairly be claimed that the penal substitutionary model embodies a richer witness to divine love than any other model of atonement, for it sees the Son at his Father's will going lower than any other view ventures to suggest. That death on the cross was a criminal's death, physically as painful as, if not more painful than, any mode of judicial execution that the world has seen; and that Jesus endured it in full consciousness of being innocent before God and man, and yet of being despised and rejected, whether in malicious conceit or in sheer fecklessness, by persons he had loved and tried to save—this is ground common to all views and tells us already that the love of Jesus, which took him to the cross, brought him appallingly low. But the penal substitution model adds to all this a further dimension of truly unimaginable distress, compared with which everything mentioned so far pales into insignificance. This is *the* dimension indicated by Denney—"that in that dark hour He had to realise to the full the divine reaction against sin in the race." Owen stated this formally, abstractly, and non-psychologically. Christ, he said, satisfied God's justice "for all the sins of all those for whom he made satisfaction, by undergoing that same punishment which, by reason of the obligation that was upon them, they were bound to undergo. When I say the same I mean essentially the same in weight and pressure, though not in all accidents of duration and the like."[43] Jonathan Edwards expressed the thought with tender and noble empathy:

> God dealt with him as if he had been exceedingly angry with him, and as though he had been the object of his dreadful wrath. This made all the sufferings of Christ the more terrible to him, because they were from the hand of his Father, whom he infinitely loved, and whose infinite love he had had eternal experience of. Besides, it was an effect of God's wrath that he forsook Christ. This caused Christ to cry out ... "My God, my God, why hast thou forsaken me?" This was infinitely terrible to Christ. Christ's knowledge of the glory of the Father, and his love to the Father, and the sense and experience he had had of the worth of his Father's love to him, made the withholding the pleasant ideas and manifestations of his Father's love as terrible to him, as the sense and knowledge of his hatred is to the damned, that have no knowledge of God's excellency, no love to him, nor any experience of the infinite sweetness of his love.[44]

And the legendary "Rabbi" Duncan concentrated it all into a single unforgettable sentence, in a famous outburst to one of his classes: "D'ye know what Calvary was? what? what? what?" Then, with tears on his face—"It was *damnation*; and he took it *lovingly*." It is precisely this love that, in the last analysis, penal substitution

43. John Owen, *Works*, 10:269. To construe Owen's statement of equivalence between what threatened us and what Christ endured in "quantitative" terms, as if some calculus of penal pain was being applied, would be a misunderstanding, though admittedly one which Owen's constant reliance on the model of payment invites, and against which he did not guard. But Denney's statement expresses what Owen means.

44. Jonathan Edwards, *Works*, ed. E. Hickman (London: Banner of Truth, 1975), 2:575. Cf. Luther: "Christ himself suffered the dread and horror of a distressed conscience that tasted eternal wrath. . . . It was not a game, or a joke, or play-acting when he said, 'Thou hast forsaken me'; for then he felt himself really forsaken in all things even as a sinner is forsaken" (*Werke*, 5:602, 605); and Calvin: "He bore in his soul the dreadful torments of a condemned and lost man" (*Inst.* 2: xvi. 10). Thus Calvin explained Christ's descent into hell: hell means Godforsakenness, and the descent took place during the hours on the cross. Jesus' cry of dereliction has been variously explained as voicing (a) depressive delusion, (b) genuine perplexity, (c) an "as if" feeling, (d) trust in God (because Jesus quotes the first words of Psalm 22, which ends with trust triumphant), (e) a repressed thought forcing its way into the open (so that the cry was a Freudian lapse), (f) a truth which Jesus wanted men to know. Surely only the last view can be taken seriously as either exegesis or theology. For a compelling discussion, cf. Leon Morris, *op. cit.*, 42–49.

is all about, and that explains its power in the lives of those who acknowledge it.[45]

What was potentially the most damaging criticism of penal substitution came not from Socinus but from McLeod Campbell, who argued that by saying that God *must* punish sin but *need not* act in mercy at all (and in fact does not act in mercy towards all), Reformed exponents of this view reduced God's love to an arbitrary decision that does not reveal his character but leaves him even in blessing us an enigma to us, "the unknown God."[46] The real target of Campbell's criticism is the Scotist model of divine personality with which, rightly or wrongly, he thought Reformed theologians worked; and a sufficient reply, from the standpoint of this lecture, would be that since the Bible says that Christ's death was a penal substitution for God's people and also that it reveals God's love to sinful men as such, and since the Bible further declares that Christ is the Father's image, so that everything we learn of the Son's love is knowledge of the Father's love also, Campbell's complaint is unreal. But Campbell's criticism, if carried, would be fatal, for any account of the atonement that fails to highlight its character as a revelation of redeeming love stands self-condemned.

The ingredients in the evangelical model of penal substitution are now, I believe, all before us, along with the task it performs. It embodies and expresses insights about the cross that are basic to personal religion, and which I therefore state in personal terms, as follows:

45. C. F. D. Moule is right to say that costly forgiving love which, in the interests of the offender's personhood, requires him to face and meet his responsibility evokes "a burning desire to make reparation and to share the burdens of the one who forgave him. . . . The original self-concern which, in the process of repentance, is transformed into a concern for the one he has injured, makes the penitent eager to lavish on the one who forgives him all that he has and is." It is certainly right to explicate God's forgiveness of our sins in terms of this model; though whether Moule is also right to dismiss God's justice non-retributively and to eliminate penal satisfaction and to dismiss New Testament references to God's wrath and punishment as atavistic survivals and "anomalies" is quite another question. "The Theology of Forgiveness," in *From Fear to Faith: Studies of Suffering and Wholeness*, ed. Norman Autton (London: SPCK, 1971), 61–72; esp. 66f., 72.

46. Op. cit., 55.

1) God, in Denney's phrase, "condones nothing," but judges all sin as it deserves: which Scripture affirms, and my conscience confirms, to be right.

2) My sins merit ultimate penal suffering and rejection from God's presence (conscience also confirms this), and nothing I do can blot them out.

3) The penalty due to me for my sins, whatever it was, was paid for me by Jesus Christ, the Son of God, in his death on the cross.

4) Because this is so, I through faith in him am made "the righteousness of God in him," i.e., I am justified; pardon, acceptance, and sonship become mine.

5) Christ's death for me is my sole ground of hope before God. "If he fulfilled not justice, I must; if he underwent not wrath, I must to eternity."[47]

6) My faith in Christ is God's own gift to me, given in virtue of Christ's death for me; i.e., the cross procured it.

7) Christ's death for me guarantees my preservation to glory.

8) Christ's death for me is the measure and pledge of the love of the Father and the Son to me.

9) Christ's death for me calls and constrains me to trust, to worship, to love, and to serve.

Thus we see what, according to this model, the cross achieved—and achieves.

47. John Owen, *Works*, 10:284.

Conclusion: The Cross in the Bible

In drawing the threads together, two general questions about the relation of the penal substitutionary model to the biblical data as a whole may be briefly considered.

1) Are the contents and functioning of this model inconsistent in any way with the faith and religion of the New Testament? Is it degrading to God, or morally offensive, as is sometimes alleged? Our analysis has, I hope, served to show that it is not any of these things. And to have shown that may not be time wasted, for it seems clear that treatments of biblical material on the atonement are often influenced by prejudices of this kind, which produce reluctance to recognize how strong is the evidence for the integral place of substitution in biblical thinking about the cross.[48]

2) Is our model truly based on the Bible? On this, several quick points may be made.

First, full weight must be given to the fact that, as Luther saw, the central question to which the whole New Testament in one way or another is addressed is the question of our relationship, here and hereafter, with our holy Creator: the question, that is, how weak, perverse, estranged, and guilty sinners may gain and guard knowledge of God's gracious pardon, acceptance and renewal. It is to this question that Christ is the answer, and that all New Testament interpretation of the cross relates.

Second, full weight must also be given to the fact that all who down the centuries have espoused this model of penal substitution have done so because they thought the Bible taught it, and scholars who for whatever reason take a different view repeatedly acknowledge that there are Bible passages that would most naturally be taken in a penal substitutionary sense. Such passages include Isaiah 53 (where Whale, as we saw, [n. 36] finds penal substitution mentioned twelve times), Galatians 3:13, 2 Corinthians 5:15, and 1 Peter 3:18; and there are many analogous to these.

Third, it must be noticed that the familiar exegetical arguments that, if accepted, erode the substitutionary view—the arguments,

---

48. See on this Leon Morris, op. cit., chap. 10, 364–419.

for instance, for a nonpersonal concept of God's wrath and a non-propitiatory understanding of the ἱλασκομαι word group, or for the interpreting of bloodshed in the Old Testament sacrifices as the release of life to invigorate rather than the ending of it to expiate—only amount to this: that certain passages may not mean quite what they have appeared to mean to Bible students of earlier generations. But at every point it remains distinctly arguable that the time-honored view is the true one, after all.

Fourth, it must be noted that there is no shortage of scholars who maintain the integral place of penal substitution in the New Testament witness to the cross. The outstanding contributions of James Denney and Leon Morris have already been mentioned, and they do not stand alone. For further illustration of this point, I subjoin two quotations from Professor A. M. Hunter. I do so without comment; they speak for themselves.

The first quotation is on the teaching of Jesus in the Synoptic Gospels. Having referred to theories of the atonement "which deal in 'satisfaction' or substitution, or make use of 'the sacrificial principle,'" Hunter proceeds:

> It is with this type of theory that the sayings of Jesus seem best to agree. There can be little doubt that Jesus viewed his death as a representative sacrifice for "the many." Not only is His thought saturated in Isa. liii (which is a doctrine of representative suffering), but His words over the cup—indeed, the whole narrative of the Last Supper—almost demand to be interpreted in terms of a sacrifice in whose virtue His followers can share. The idea of substitution which is prominent in Isa. liii appears in the ransom saying. And it requires only a little reading between the lines to find in the "cup" saying, the story of the Agony, and the cry of dereliction, evidence that Christ's sufferings were what, for lack of a better word, we can only call "penal."[49]

The second quotation picks up comments on what, by common consent, are Paul's two *loci classici* on the method of atonement, 2 Corinthians 5:21 and Galatians 3:13. On the first, Hunter writes:

49. A. M. Hunter, *The Words and Works of Jesus* (London: SCM, 1950), 100.

Paul declares that the crucified Christ, on our behalf, took the whole reality of sin upon himself, like the scapegoat: "For our sake he made him to be sin who knew no sin, so that in him we might become the righteousness of God." Paul sees the Cross as an act of God's doing in which the Sinless One, for the sake of sinners, somehow experienced the horror of the divine reaction against sin so that there might be condemnation no more.

Gal. 3:13 moves in the same realm of ideas. "Christ redeemed us from the curse of the law, having become a curse for us." [I interpose here my own comment, that Paul's aorist participle is explaining the method of redemption, answering the question "how did Christ redeem us?" and might equally well therefore be translated "*by becoming* a curse for us."] The curse is the divine condemnation of sin which leads to death. To this curse we lay exposed; but Christ on his cross identified himself with the doom impending on sinners that, through his act, the curse passes away and we go free.

Such passages show the holy love of God taking awful issue in the cross with the sin of man. Christ, by God's appointing, dies the sinner's death, and so removes sin. Is there a simpler way of saying this than that Christ bore our sins? We are not fond nowadays of calling Christ's suffering "penal" or of styling him our "substitute"; but can we avoid using some such words as these to express Paul's view of the atonement?[50]

Well, can we? And if not, what follows? Can we then justify ourselves in holding a view of the atonement into which penal substitution does not enter? Ought we not to reconsider whether penal substitution is not, after all, the heart of the matter? These are among the questions that our preliminary survey in this lecture has raised. It is to be hoped that they will receive the attention they deserve.

50. A. M. Hunter, *Interpreting Paul's Gospel* (London: SCM, 1954), 31f.

3

Nothing but the Blood

Mark Dever

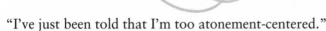

"I've just been told that I'm too atonement-centered."

My sister in Christ was serious, humble, and a little confused. I said, "What do you mean 'too atonement-centered'?" I had never heard the charge.

A Christian friend told her that she talked too much about Christ's death, which dealt with our guilt due to sin. I responded that knowing and accepting this truth was the only way to a relationship with God, and that I didn't think it was possible to be "too atonement-centered."

Few other doctrines go to the heart of the Christian faith like the atonement. Congregations sing at the top of their lungs: "My sin, not in part but the whole, has been nailed to the cross, so I bear it no more, praise the Lord, praise the Lord, O my soul!" The priestly work of Christ separates Christianity from Judaism and Islam. Not surprisingly, the cross has become the symbol for our faith.

Still, God's work on the cross leaves us with plenty of questions. In fact, there have always been a few Christians who question whether we need the atonement, including, in recent years, some evangelicals who have challenged the dominant understanding of Christ's death on the cross as the substitute for our sins.

At stake is nothing less than the essence of Christianity. Historically understood, Christ's atonement gives hope to Christians in their sin and in their suffering. If we have any assurance of salvation, it is because of Christ's atonement; if any joy, it flows from Christ's work on the cross. The atonement protects us from our native tendency to replace religion with morality and God's grace with legalism. Apart from Christ's atoning work, we would be forever guilty, ashamed, and condemned before God. But not everyone these days sees it that way.

Different Crosses

Christians have understood the Bible's abundant atonement language and imagery by means of various theories. J. I. Packer, in his classic 1973 lecture, "What Did the Cross Achieve? The Logic of Penal Substitution,"[1] outlined three sets of theories, or visions. Each vision sees humanity's main problem differently, and each theory explains how Christ's death solves that problem.

The first set of theories argues that humanity's main problem is that we are trapped and oppressed by spiritual forces beyond our control. Christ's death, then, is seen as a ransom that frees us from captivity. His death and resurrection defeat the evil spiritual forces. These theories are generally summarized under the heading of ransom theory or *Christus Victor* (Christ the Victor).

The second set of theories deals with the subjective need of all people to know God's love for us. These theories emphasize that Christ's death on the Cross demonstrates God's love so dramatically that we are convinced of his love and are now able to share it with others. This set includes the moral-influence theory of Abelard, among others.

A third set of theories assumes that our main problem is God's righteous wrath against us for our sinfulness, which puts us in danger of eternal punishment. These theories argue that Christ's perfect

1. Packer's lecture appears as chapter 2 of this volume.

sacrifice for our sins is necessary to satisfy God's righteousness. Christ's death bore a divine penalty that we deserved. By taking our penalty upon himself, God satisfied his own correct and good wrath against us. Theories in this set, such as the satisfaction theory and the penal-substitution theory, emphasize how Christ represents us.

The new wave of criticism has targeted this last set of theories, especially the view of Christ as a penal substitute—a theory long central for most Protestant groups, especially evangelicals. The criticism follows a path laid by others throughout history, from Abelard to Socinus to Schleiermacher to C. H. Dodd. In 1955, English Methodist theologian Vincent Taylor noted the "clearly marked . . . tendency to reject theories of substitutionary punishment." Roman Catholic dissenters have turned from emphasizing the cultic rituals of sacrifice to the ethics of imitating Christ's sacrifice. In Lutheran circles, Gustav Aulén's *Christus Victor* (1931) led the charge to replace a substitutionary understanding of the atonement with what he called the "classical" understanding—Christ as liberating us from spiritual forces that have enslaved us.

Hearing the Critics

Critics, past and present, usually raise four main objections to substitutionary atonement.

1) Not Enough?

Many current mainline Christians—such as William Placher in "Christ Takes Our Place" (*Interpretation*, January 1999), and Peter Schmiechen in *Saving Power* (Eerdmans, 2005)—say that penal substitution is, at best, inadequate. They say the true focus of atonement doctrine lies beyond achieving forgiveness.

For example, Stephen Finlan represents the stream of Christian thought following Abelard and Schleiermacher that stresses the incarnation rather than any particular understanding of the atonement. In his dissertation, *The Backgrounds and Content of Paul's Cultic Atonement Metaphors* (Brill, 2004), and in his book *Problems with Atonement* (Liturgical Press, 2005), he sees the whole framework of "satisfaction" as medieval, coming to us not from Paul, but from Anselm. Finlan acknowledges that "sacrifice" and "scapegoat" are images rooted in the Old Testament, images that Paul and the writer of Hebrews use, but he says only later theologizing led Christians to theorize about the atonement. In the end, Finlan concludes that Christians should realize that the atonement is secondary to the incarnation. He argues that we should think about atonement as *theosis*, as growing in Godlike spirituality and conduct, thus sharing in the life of God.

The Eastern Orthodox have long accepted *theosis* as the main result of Christ's death. Reflecting on 2 Corinthians 3:18, Ephesians 4:13, 2 Peter 1:4, and other passages, many have suggested that God's work in us through Christ is best understood not by language of penalty, payment, ransom, and satisfaction, but by language of love, inclusion, growth, and deification. Seen this way, the church becomes an extension of the incarnation of God in Christ, and biblical images of the church as the body of Christ take on a more realistic hue.

2) Irrelevant?

Other critics, concerned with clearly communicating the gospel, charge that substitution does not make sense to modern cultures, does not mesh with most of what is in the Gospels, and glorifies unforgiving, abusive behavior. Joel Green and Mark Baker, in *Recovering the Scandal of the Cross* (InterVarsity, 2000), say, "We believe that the popular fascination with and commitment to penal substitutionary Atonement has had ill effects in the life of the church in the United States and has little to offer the global church and mission by way of understanding or embodying the message of Jesus Christ." Such critics argue that modern cultures, which are far removed from religions that offer blood sacrifices, find substitutionary theory irrelevant and distasteful.

3) Individualistic?

Green and Baker also argue that penal substitution has encouraged individualism, because it seems to focus on individual guilt and forgiveness. As such, say these critics, it has blinded the church to social issues like materialism, racism, and nationalism. British scholar James D. G. Dunn has argued, "[Substitution] smacks too much of individualism to represent Paul's thought adequately."

4) Too Violent?

Perhaps the most powerful criticism of penal substitution has come from a swelling chorus of scholars who decry its violence. Inspired by French scholar René Girard, many modern theologians have denied the need for divine violence as part of redemption. They reject God's apparent double standard in doing what he forbids others to do—take life.

Roman Catholics have debated this last point for thirty years. But only recently has this concern penetrated evangelicalism, steeped as it is in the substitution-rich language of Watts's and Wesley's hymns. Some evangelicals have taken to the work of Anthony Bartlett, J. Denny Weaver, Steve Chalke, and Alan Mann, who decry the language of violence in substitutionary atonement. Two years after publishing his controversial book *The Lost Message of Jesus* (Zondervan, 2004), Chalke wrote, "The church's inability to shake off the great distortion of God contained in the theory of penal substitution, with its inbuilt belief in retribution and the redemptive power of violence, has cost us dearly." Chalke and others say that substitution, at worst, produces a twisted justification of violence and encourages selfish, individualistic abuses of power.

Green and Baker warn against suggesting that God the Father did something to God the Son. In popular church discourse, sermon illustrations of Christ's sacrifice on the cross have fueled complaints about substitution. For example, there is the story of the railroad operator who learns that the bridge ahead is out, so he prepares to switch the tracks to save the lives of hundreds on a fast-approaching train. But at that moment, he sees his son playing in the gears, and he pauses to reconsider. Here, many a preacher has meditated on God's love in ways that border on the grotesque—we're told that the man decided to go ahead and sacrifice his son's life in order to save those on the train. Such an unwitting sacrifice has led to the charge that the atonement is divine child abuse.

Substitutionary Scriptures

Substitutionary atonement has indeed been misapplied. The railroad analogy above, for example, is inadequate because it does not include the Holy Spirit. But even more to the point, Christ willingly offered up his life; he was not blindsided by the cross. And the Bible does include many different ways of talking about Christ's death. But it remains odd how many writers these days downplay or even deny the doctrine of penal substitution, because it is the dominant atonement imagery used in the Bible. The following paragraphs may be a bit Bible heavy for some readers, but I include them to demonstrate how central this theme is to the scriptural witness—and I'm barely scratching the surface.

The regulations for Israel laid out in the book of Exodus, for example, frequently mention atonement being made for the people by means of sacrificial bloodshed. The regulations assume that God is holy and that people owe God obedience. Thus, action is needed to facilitate a peaceful, reconciled relationship. But these atonements were things that people did, following God's command.

The writer of Hebrews referred to these sacrifices and said that the law "can never, by the same sacrifices repeated endlessly year after year, make perfect those who draw near to worship. If it could, would they not have stopped being offered? For the worshipers would have been cleansed once for all, and would no longer have felt guilty for their sins. But those sacrifices are an annual reminder of sins, because it is impossible for the blood of bulls and goats to take away sins" (Heb. 10:1–4).[2]

Against this background, God says to his people in exile, "Then, when I make atonement for you for all you have done . . ." (Ezek. 16:63). How would God do that?

In Hebrews 2:17 we read, "For this reason [Jesus] had to be made like his brothers in every way, in order that he might become a merciful and

2. Unless otherwise noted, Scripture quotations used in this chapter are taken from the New International Version (NIV).

faithful high priest in service to God, and that he might make atonement [*hilaskesthai* in the Greek original] for the sins of the people."

Paul's statement in Romans 3:25 is another crucial atonement text: "God presented him as a sacrifice of atonement, through faith in his blood." Again, the word "atonement" is related to the verb for "propitiate" or "atone," *hilasterion*. Recent commentators have continued to differ over the best interpretation of the word, but all agree that some sort of substitution is indicated. Douglas Moo of Wheaton College Graduate School affirmed that "sacrifice of atonement" is a good rendering—neither too restrictive nor too vague. Thomas Schreiner of Southern Baptist Theological Seminary prefers "propitiation" in order to retain a clear reference to God's wrath, which is alluded to in the preceding chapters of Paul's argument.

Such language is not limited to Paul. The apostle John, too, refers to Christ's death as an *hilasmos* (1 John 2:2 and 4:10), an atoning sacrifice or propitiation.

The New Testament also includes bloody images of sacrifice and religious ritual (Eph. 2:13; Col. 1:20; Rom. 5:9–10). Such images remind us that Christ accomplished something with his physical death. Other atonement language borrows economic images from the marketplace and the prison, where something is purchased or redeemed for a price (Luke 24:21; Gal. 4:5; Titus 2:14).

The language of propitiation specifically implies God's hatred of sin and emphasizes the gracious work of Christ as sin bearer (Rom. 3:25). The Bible further includes the forensic, legal language of justification (Rom. 3:20–26; 4:25; 5:16–18). These images make clear the reality of our guilt and the required penalty.

Yes, relational language is also used to describe the effects of Christ's death (Rom. 5:8–10), but often with substitutionary overtones: God has reconciled us, dealing with the barrier of hostility between himself and humanity by means of Christ's death (2 Corinthians 5).

Even the language of warfare and victory (John 16:33; Col. 2:15) is imbued with substitutionary overtones. These passages recognize the reality of the spiritual struggle that we are involved in and present Christ's death on our behalf as a crucial element in God's victory.

Problems with Problems

Many critics of substitution get around this "problem"—that such language and imagery is found everywhere in the Bible—by downplaying its importance or reinterpreting it in ways that I believe do violence to the plain meaning of the text. Scot McKnight, for example, in his recent *Jesus and His Death* (Baylor, 2005), does lots of careful work with the Gospel text. Nonetheless, he assumes that the last phrase in Mark 10:45—"For even the Son of Man did not come to be served but to serve, and to give his life as a ransom for many"—reports not Jesus' original words but Mark's theologizing. And while admitting that the idea of substitution is strongly suggested here, he finally rejects it.

Further, McKnight uses Christ's words to interpret atonement passages in Paul, Peter, and Hebrews—even though the Epistles provide the most sustained discussions of Christ's atonement. He again acknowledges that such passages might carry along with them "the notions of penal substitution and satisfaction" but in the end says, "[they] need not." Thus he goes to what seem to be great lengths to avoid the plain meaning of these passages. At one point he says that Jesus is "both representative and substitute," but his interpretation so transforms the idea of substitute as to rob it of its traditional theological meaning.

Stephen Finlan also seems to pit one portion of Scripture against another. He writes in *Problems with Atonement*, "It is a mistake to identify Atonement as the central Christian doctrine, although it is central to the Pauline tradition, to First Peter, Hebrews, First John, and Revelation. But these books in their entirety compose only 39 percent of the New Testament."

Even if one were to grant Finlan's premise (which I certainly don't), 39 percent of the New Testament can hardly be swept away or ignored. For those of us who maintain that the apostles' writings bear equal authority to Jesus' words in the Gospels—and that they are themselves inspired by the Spirit of Jesus (see John 16:12–15)—substitutionary, sin-bearing language must be accepted as the dominant atonement metaphor in the Bible.

Many-splendored Atonement

Still, why pit these theories against each other and discount, ignore, or diminish biblical language that describes the death of Christ? While a victor may have moral influence on those for whom he conquered, may he not also be a substitute? While Christ's example of self-giving love may also defeat our enemies, may he not, by the same act, propitiate God's wrath? Each of the theories conveys biblical truth about the atoning work of Christ.

I don't doubt that we have more to learn from Christ's death than simply the fact that he died as a substitute for us, bearing our grief and carrying our sorrows (Isa. 53:4). Peter, for instance, teaches that we should follow Christ's example of suffering for that which is good (1 Peter 3). Any biblical understanding of the atonement must take into account our having been united to Christ by faith, adopted and regenerated in him. As those who belong to him, as his temple and his body, we expect the fruit of his Spirit to be evident in us. Because of the atonement, we expect a new quality to our lives (Romans 6; 2 Corinthians 5; Galatians 5; 2 Peter 1). The atonement is not merely moral influence, but it surely results in moral improvement.

Rather than pitting these theories against one another, couldn't they be evaluated together? A Christ who wins victory over the powers of evil, whose death changes us, and whose death propitiates God is not only conceivable, but he seems to be the Bible's composite presentation. Frank Thielman of Beeson Divinity School states a traditional view of the atonement in his recent summary, *Theology of the New Testament* (Zondervan, 2005). But Thielman, a scholar who has focused his work more on Paul than on the Gospels, also presents the cross as a defeat of those cosmic powers opposing God—*Christus Victor*. As Hans Boersma wrote of atonement theories in *Books & Culture* (March/April, 2003), "By allowing the entire choir to sing together, I suspect we may end up serving the interests of God's eschatological *shalom*."

Still, when we give attention and authority to all parts of the New Testament canon, substitution becomes the center and focus of the Bible's witness to the meaning of Christ's death, and the measure of

God's redeeming love. As New Testament theologian George Eldon Ladd said, "The objective and substitutionary character of the death of Christ as the supreme demonstration of God's love should result in a transformation of conduct that is effected by the constraining power of that love." Theologian Donald Bloesch is in line with this when he insists: "Evangelical theology affirms the vicarious, substitutionary Atonement of Jesus Christ. It does not claim that this theory does justice to all aspects of Christ's atoning work, but it does see substitution as the heart of the Atonement."

No Sacrifice Too Great

And what about that charge of being "too atonement-centered"? We must center our lives around Christ's atonement. We don't want to encourage violence, marginalize the gospel, or promote individualistic passivity. But I haven't seen sinners who are gripped by Christ's substitutionary death respond that way. Instead, I've more often observed responses like C. T. Studd's famous statement: "If Jesus Christ be God, and died for me, then no sacrifice can be too great for me to make for him." Charles Spurgeon put that point well: "It is our duty and our privilege to exhaust our lives for Jesus. We are not to be living specimens of men in fine preservation, but living *sacrifices*, whose lot is to be consumed."

In C. J. Mahaney's book *Living the Cross Centered Life* (Multnomah, 2006), he shares with us his advice to his young son, Chad: "This is what I hold out to my young son as the hope of his life: that Jesus, God's perfect, righteous Son, died in his place for his sins. Jesus took all the punishment; Jesus received all the wrath as he hung on the Cross, so people like Chad and his sinful daddy could be completely forgiven." Like Chad, we would do well to accept our guilt and admire God's grace, to let the Holy Spirit encourage us by the Savior's self-denying love to follow his example, and to savor God's love to us in this almost incredible sacrifice.

4

Saved by His Precious Blood

An Introduction to John Owen's
The Death of Death in the Death of Christ

J. I. Packer

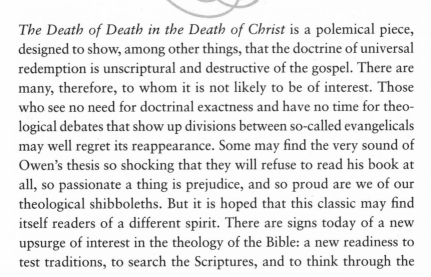

The Death of Death in the Death of Christ is a polemical piece, designed to show, among other things, that the doctrine of universal redemption is unscriptural and destructive of the gospel. There are many, therefore, to whom it is not likely to be of interest. Those who see no need for doctrinal exactness and have no time for theological debates that show up divisions between so-called evangelicals may well regret its reappearance. Some may find the very sound of Owen's thesis so shocking that they will refuse to read his book at all, so passionate a thing is prejudice, and so proud are we of our theological shibboleths. But it is hoped that this classic may find itself readers of a different spirit. There are signs today of a new upsurge of interest in the theology of the Bible: a new readiness to test traditions, to search the Scriptures, and to think through the faith. It is to those who share this readiness that Owen's treatise is now offered, in the belief that it will help us in one of the most urgent tasks facing evangelical Christendom today—the recovery of the gospel.

This last remark may cause some raising of eyebrows, but it seems to be warranted by the facts.

There is no doubt that evangelicalism today is in a state of perplexity and unsettlement. In such matters as the practice of evangelism, the teaching of holiness, the building up of local church life, the pastor's dealing with souls, and the exercise of discipline, there is evidence of widespread dissatisfaction with things as they are and of equally widespread uncertainty as to the road ahead. This is a complex phenomenon to which many factors have contributed; but, if we go to the root of the matter, we shall find that these perplexities are all ultimately due to our having lost our grip on the biblical gospel. Without realizing it, we have during the past century bartered that gospel for a substitute product which, though it looks similar enough in points of detail, is as a whole a decidedly different thing. Hence our troubles; for the substitute product does not answer the ends for which the authentic gospel has in past days proved itself so mighty. Why?

We would suggest that the reason lies in its own character and content. It fails to make men God-centered in their thoughts and God-fearing in their hearts because this is not primarily what it is trying to do. One way of stating the difference between it and the old gospel is to say that it is too exclusively concerned to be "helpful" to man—to bring peace, comfort, happiness, satisfaction—and too little concerned to glorify God. The old gospel was "helpful," too—more so, indeed, than is the new—but (so to speak) incidentally, for its first concern was always to give glory to God. It was always and essentially a proclamation of divine sovereignty in mercy and judgment, a summons to bow down and worship the mighty Lord on whom man depends for all good, both in nature and in grace. Its center of reference was unambiguously God. But in the new gospel the center of reference is man. This is just to say

112

that the old gospel was *religious* in a way that the new gospel is not. Whereas the chief aim of the old was to teach men to worship God, the concern of the new seems limited to making them feel better. The subject of the old gospel was God and his ways with men; the subject of the new is man and the help God gives him. There is a world of difference. The whole perspective and emphasis of gospel preaching has changed.

From this change of interest has sprung a change of content, for the new gospel has in effect reformulated the biblical message in the supposed interests of "helpfulness." Accordingly, the themes of man's natural inability to believe, of God's free election being the ultimate cause of salvation, and of Christ dying specifically for his sheep are not preached. These doctrines, it would be said, are not "helpful"; they would drive sinners to despair by suggesting to them that it is not in their own power to be saved through Christ. (The possibility that such despair might be salutary is not considered; it is taken for granted that it cannot be, because it is so shattering to our self-esteem.) However this may be (and we shall say more about it later), the result of these omissions is that part of the biblical gospel is now preached as if it were the whole of that gospel; and a half-truth masquerading as the whole truth becomes a complete untruth. Thus, we appeal to men as if they all had the ability to receive Christ at any time; we speak of his redeeming work as if he had done no more by dying than make it possible for us to save ourselves by believing; we speak of God's love as if it were no more than a general willingness to receive any who will turn and trust; and we depict the Father and the Son, not as sovereignly active in drawing sinners to themselves, but as waiting in quiet impotence "at the door of our hearts" for us to let them in.

It is undeniable that this is how we preach; perhaps this is what we really believe. But it needs to be said with emphasis that this set of twisted half-truths is something other than the biblical gospel. The Bible is against us when we preach in this way; and the fact that such preaching has become almost standard practice among us only shows how urgent it is that we should review this matter. To recover the old, authentic, biblical gospel, and to bring our preaching and practice back into line with it, is perhaps our most pressing present need. And it is at this point that Owen's treatise on redemption can give us help.

Calvinism Defined

"But wait a minute," says someone; "it's all very well to talk like this about the gospel; but surely what Owen is doing is defending limited atonement—one of the five points of Calvinism? When you speak of recovering the gospel, don't you mean that you just want us all to become Calvinists?"

These questions are worth considering, for they will no doubt occur to many. At the same time, however, they are questions that reflect a great deal of prejudice and ignorance. "Defending limited atonement"—as if this was all that a Reformed theologian expounding the heart of the gospel could ever really want to do! "You just want us all to become Calvinists"—as if Reformed theologians had no interest beyond recruiting for their party, and as if becoming a Calvinist was the last stage of theological depravity, and had nothing to do with the gospel at all. Before we answer these questions directly, we must try to remove the prejudices that underlie them by making clear what Calvinism really is; and therefore we would ask the reader to take note of the following facts, historical and theological, about Calvinism in general and the "five points" in particular.

First, it should be observed that the "five points of Calvinism," so-called, are simply the Calvinistic answer to a five-point manifesto (the Remonstrance) put out by certain "Belgic semi-Pelagians"[1] in the early seventeenth century. The theology that it contained (known to history as Arminianism) stemmed from two philosophical principles: first, that divine sovereignty is not compatible with human freedom, nor therefore with human responsibility; second, that ability limits obligation. (The charge of semi-Pelagianism was thus fully justified.) From these principles, the Arminians drew two deductions: first,

1. John Owen, *Works*, 10:6.

that since the Bible regards faith as a free and responsible human act, it cannot be caused by God but is exercised independently of him; second, that since the Bible regards faith as obligatory on the part of all who hear the gospel, ability to believe must be universal. Hence, they maintained, Scripture must be interpreted as teaching the following positions: (1) Man is never so completely corrupted by sin that he cannot savingly believe the gospel when it is put before him, nor (2) is he ever so completely controlled by God that he cannot reject it. (3) God's election of those who shall be saved is prompted by his foreseeing that they will of their own accord believe. (4) Christ's death did not ensure the salvation of anyone, for it did not secure the gift of faith to anyone (there is no such gift); what it did was rather to create a possibility of salvation for everyone if they believe. (5) It rests with believers to keep themselves in a state of grace by keeping up their faith; those who fail here fall away and are lost. Thus, Arminianism made man's salvation depend ultimately on man himself, saving faith being viewed throughout as man's own work and, because his own, not God's in him.

The Synod of Dort was convened in 1618 to pronounce on this theology, and the "five points of Calvinism" represent its counter-affirmations. They stem from a very different principle—the biblical principle that "salvation is of the Lord" (Jonah 2:9 KJV); and they may be summarized thus: (1) Fallen man in his natural state lacks all power to believe the gospel, just as he lacks all power to believe the law, despite all external inducements that may be extended to him. (2) God's election is a free, sovereign, unconditional choice of sinners, as sinners, to be redeemed by Christ, given faith, and brought to glory. (3) The redeeming work of Christ had as its end and goal the salvation of the elect. (4) The work of the Holy Spirit in bringing men to faith never fails to achieve its object. (5) Believers are kept in faith and grace by the unconquerable power of God till they come to glory. These five points are conveniently denoted by the mnemonic TULIP: Total depravity, Unconditional election, Limited atonement, Irresistible grace, Preservation of the saints.

115

Now, here are two coherent interpretations of the biblical gospel, which stand in evident opposition to each other. The difference between them is not primarily one of emphasis, but of content. One proclaims a God who saves; the other speaks of a God who enables man to save himself. One view presents the three great acts of the holy Trinity for the recovering of lost mankind—election by the Father, redemption by the Son, calling by the Spirit—as directed toward the same persons, and as securing their salvation infallibly. The other view gives each act a different reference (the objects of redemption being all mankind, of calling, those who hear the gospel, and of election, those hearers who respond), and denies that any man's salvation is secured by any of them. The two theologies thus conceive the plan of salvation in quite different terms. One makes salvation depend on the work of God, the other on a work of man; one regards faith as part of God's gift of salvation, the other as man's own contribution to salvation; one gives all the glory of saving believers to God, the other divides the praise between God, who, so to speak, built the machinery of salvation, and man, who by believing operated it. Plainly, these differences are important, and the permanent value of the "five points," as a summary of Calvinism, is that they make clear the points at which, and the extent to which, these two conceptions are at variance.

However, it would not be correct simply to equate Calvinism with the "five points." Five points of our own will make this clear.

In the first place, Calvinism is something much broader than the "five points" indicate. Calvinism is a whole worldview, stemming from a clear vision of God as the whole world's Maker and King. Calvinism is the consistent endeavor to acknowledge the Creator as the Lord, working all things after the counsel of his will. Calvinism is a theocentric way of thinking about all life under the direction and control of God's own Word. Calvinism, in other words, is the theology of the Bible viewed from the perspective of the Bible—the God-centered outlook that sees the Creator as the source and means and end of everything that is, both in nature and in grace. Calvinism is thus theism (belief in God as the ground of all things), religion (dependence on God as the giver of all things), and evangelicalism (trust in God through Christ for all things), all in their purest and most highly developed form. And Calvinism is a unified philosophy of history that sees the whole diversity of processes and events that take place in God's world as no more, and no less, than the outworking of his great preordained plan for his creatures and his church. The five points assert no more than that God is sovereign in saving the individual, but Calvinism, as such, is concerned with the much broader assertion that he is sovereign everywhere.

Then, in the second place, the "five points" present Calvinistic soteriology in a negative and polemical form, whereas Calvinism in itself is essentially expository, pastoral, and constructive. It can define its position in terms of Scripture without any reference to Arminianism, and it does not need to be forever fighting real or imaginary Arminians in order to keep itself alive. Calvinism has no interest in negatives, as such; when Calvinists fight, they fight for positive evangelical values. The negative cast of the "five points" is misleading chiefly with regard to the third (limited atonement, or particular redemption), which is often read with stress on the adjective and taken as indicating that Calvinists have a special interest in confining the limits of divine mercy. But in fact the purpose of this phraseology, as we shall see, is to safeguard the central affirmation of the gospel—that Christ is a Redeemer who really does redeem. Similarly, the denials of an election that is conditional and of grace that is resistible are intended to safeguard the positive truth that it is God who saves. The real negations are those of Arminianism, which denies that election, redemption, and calling are saving acts of God. Calvinism negates these negations in order to assert the positive content of the gospel, for the positive purpose of strengthening faith and building up the church.

Thirdly, the very act of setting out Calvinistic soteriology in the form of five distinct points (a number due, as we saw, merely to the fact that there were five Arminian points for the Synod of Dort to answer) tends to obscure the organic character of Calvinistic thought on this subject. For the five points, though separately stated, are really inseparable. They hang together; you cannot reject one without rejecting them all, at least in the sense in which the Synod meant them. For to Calvinism there is really only *one* point to be made in the field of soteriology: the point that *God saves sinners*.

God: the triune Jehovah—Father, Son, and Spirit; three Persons working together in sovereign wisdom, power, and love to achieve the salvation of a chosen people, the Father electing, the Son fulfilling the Father's will by redeeming, the Spirit executing the purpose of Father and Son by renewing. *Saves*: does everything, first to last, that is involved in bringing man from death in sin to life in glory: plans, achieves, and communicates redemption, calls and keeps, justifies, sanctifies, glorifies.

Sinners: men as God finds them, guilty, vile, helpless, powerless, blind, unable to lift a finger to do God's will or better their spiritual lot. *God saves sinners*—and the force of this confession may not be weakened by disrupting the unity of the work of the Trinity, or by dividing the achievement of salvation between God and man and making the decisive part man's own, or by soft-pedaling the sinner's inability so as to allow him to share the praise of his salvation with his Savior. This is the one point of Calvinistic soteriology that the "five points" are concerned to establish and Arminianism in all its forms to deny: namely, that sinners do not save themselves in any sense at all, but that salvation, first and last, whole and entire, past, present, and future, is of the Lord, to whom be glory for ever, amen!

This leads to our fourth remark, which is this: the five-point formula obscures the depth of the difference between Calvinistic and Arminian soteriology. There seems no doubt that it seriously misleads many here. In the formula, the stress falls on the adjectives, and this naturally gives the impression that in regard to the three great saving acts of God the debate concerns the adjectives merely—that both sides agree as to what election, redemption, and the gift of internal grace are, and differ only as to the position of man in relation to them: whether the first is conditional upon faith being foreseen or not; whether the second intends the salvation of every man or not; whether the third always proves invincible or not. But this is a complete misconception. The change of adjective in each case involves changing the meaning of the noun. An election that is conditional, a redemption that is universal, an internal grace that is resistible is not the same kind of election, redemption, internal grace that Calvinism asserts. The real issue concerns not the appropriateness of adjectives but the definition of nouns. Both sides saw this clearly when the controversy first began, and it is important that we should see it too, for otherwise we cannot discuss the Calvinist-Arminian debate to any purpose at all. It is worth setting out the different definitions side by side.

1) God's act of election was defined by the Arminians as a resolve to receive to sonship and glory a duly qualified class of people: believers in Christ.[2] This becomes a resolve to receive individual persons only in virtue of God's foreseeing the contingent fact that they will of their own accord believe. There is nothing in the decree of election to ensure that the class of believers will ever have any members; God does not determine to make any man believe. But Calvinists define election as a choice of particular undeserving persons to be saved from sin and brought to glory, and to that end to be redeemed by the death of Christ and given faith by the Spirit's effectual calling. Where the Arminian says: "I owe my election to my faith," the Calvinist says: "I owe my faith to my election." Clearly, these two concepts of election are very far apart.

2) Christ's work of redemption was defined by the Arminians as the removing of an obstacle (the unsatisfied claims of justice) that stood in the way of God's offering pardon to sinners, as he desired to do, on condition that they believe. Redemption, according to Arminianism, secured for God a right to make this offer but did not of itself ensure that anyone would ever accept it; for faith, being a work of man's own, is not a gift that comes to him from Calvary. Christ's death created an opportunity for the exercise of saving faith, but that is all it did. Calvinists, however, define redemption as Christ's actual substitutionary endurance of the penalty of sin in the place of

2. Plus any others who, though they had not heard the gospel, lived up to the light they had—though this point need not concern us here.

certain specified sinners, through which God was reconciled to them, their liability to punishment was for ever destroyed, and a title to eternal life was secured for them. In consequence of this, they now have in God's sight a right to the gift of faith, as the means of entry into the enjoyment of their inheritance. Calvary, in other words, not merely made possible the salvation of those for whom Christ died; it ensured that they would be brought to faith and their salvation made actual. The cross *saves*. Where the Arminian will say only: "I could not have gained my salvation without Calvary," the Calvinist will say: "Christ gained my salvation for me at Calvary." The former makes the cross the *sine qua non* of salvation; the latter sees it as the actual procuring cause of salvation, and traces the source of every spiritual blessing, faith included, back to the great transaction between God and his Son carried through on Calvary's hill. Clearly, these two concepts of redemption are quite at variance.

3) The Spirit's gift of internal grace was defined by the Arminians as "moral suasion," the bare bestowal of an understanding of God's truth. This, they granted—indeed, insisted—does not of itself ensure that anyone will ever make the response of faith. But Calvinists define this gift as not merely an enlightening but also as a regenerating work of God in men, "taking away their heart of stone, and giving unto them a heart of flesh; renewing their wills, and by His almighty power determining them to that which is good; and effectually drawing them to Jesus Christ; yet so as they come most freely, being made willing by his grace."[3] Grace proves irresistible just because it destroys the disposition to resist. Where the Arminian, therefore, will be content to say, "I decided for Christ," "I made up my mind to be a Christian," the Calvinist will wish to speak of his conversion in more theological fashion, to make plain whose work it really was:

> Long my imprisoned spirit lay
>   Fast bound in sin and nature's night:
>   Thine eye diffused a quickening ray;
>   I woke; the dungeon flamed with light;

3. *Westminster Confession*, 10:1.

My chains fell off: my heart was free:
I rose, went forth, and followed thee.[4]

Clearly, these two notions of internal grace are sharply opposed to each other.

Now, the Calvinist contends that the Arminian idea of election, redemption, and calling as acts of God which do not save cuts at the very heart of their biblical meaning; that to say in the Arminian sense that God elects believers, and Christ died for all men, and the Spirit quickens those who receive the Word, is really to say that in the biblical sense God elects nobody, and Christ died for nobody, and the Spirit quickens nobody. The matter at issue in this controversy, therefore, is the meaning to be given to these biblical terms, and to some others that are also soteriologically significant, such as the love of God, the covenant of grace, and the verb *save* itself, with its synonyms. Arminians gloss them all in terms of the principle that salvation does not directly depend on any decree or act of God, but on man's independent activity in believing. Calvinists maintain that this principle is itself unscriptural and irreligious, and that such glossing demonstrably perverts the sense of Scripture and undermines the gospel at every point where it is practiced. This, and nothing less than this, is what the Arminian controversy is about.

There is a fifth way in which the five-point formula is deficient. Its very form (a series of denials of Arminian assertions) lends color to the impression that Calvinism is a modification of Arminianism; that Arminianism has a certain primacy in order of nature, and developed Calvinism is an offshoot from it. Even when one shows this to be false as a matter of history, the suspicion remains in many minds that it is a true account of the relation of the two views themselves. For it is widely supposed that Arminianism (which, as we now see, corresponds pretty closely to the new gospel of our own day) is the result of reading the Scriptures in a "natural," unbiased, unsophisticated way, and that Calvinism is an unnatural growth,

---

4. Granted, it was Charles Wesley who wrote this, but it is one of the many passages in his hymns which make one ask, with "Rabbi" Duncan, "Where's your Arminianism now, friend?"

the product less of the texts themselves than of unhallowed logic working on the texts, wresting their plain sense and upsetting their balance by forcing them into a systematic framework that they do not themselves provide.

Whatever may have been true of individual Calvinists, as a generalization about Calvinism nothing could be further from the truth than this. Certainly, Arminianism is "natural" in one sense, in that it represents a characteristic perversion of biblical teaching by the fallen mind of man, who even in salvation cannot bear to renounce the delusion of being master of his fate and captain of his soul. This perversion appeared before in the Pelagianism and semi-Pelagianism of the patristic period and the later scholasticism and has recurred since the seventeenth century both in Roman theology and, among Protestants, in various types of rationalistic liberalism and modern evangelical teaching; and no doubt it will always be with us. As long as the fallen human mind is what it is, the Arminian way of thinking will continue to be a natural type of mistake. But it is not natural in any other sense. In fact, it is Calvinism that understands the Scriptures in their natural, one would have thought inescapable, meaning; Calvinism that keeps to what they actually say; Calvinism that insists on taking seriously the biblical assertions that God saves, and that he saves those whom he has chosen to save, and that he saves them by grace without works, so that no man may boast, and that Christ is given to them as a perfect Savior, and that their whole salvation flows to them from the cross, and that the work of redeeming them was finished on the cross. It is Calvinism that gives due honor to the cross. When the Calvinist sings,

> There is a green hill far away,
> Without a city wall,
> Where the dear Lord was crucified,
> *Who died to save us all;*
> *He died that we might be forgiven,*
> He died to make us good;
> *That we might go at last to Heaven,*
> Saved by His precious blood . . .

122

he means it. He will not gloss the italicized statements by saying that God's saving purpose in the death of his Son was a mere ineffectual wish, depending for its fulfillment on man's willingness to believe, so that for all God could do Christ might have died and none been saved at all. He insists that the Bible sees the cross as revealing God's power to save, not his impotence. Christ did not win a hypothetical salvation for hypothetical believers, a mere possibility of salvation for any who might possibly believe, but a real salvation for his own chosen people. His precious blood really does "save us all"; the intended effects of his self-offering do in fact follow, just because the cross was what it was. Its saving power does not depend on faith being added to it; its saving power is such that faith flows from it. The cross secured the full salvation of all for whom Christ died. "God forbid," therefore, "that I should glory, save in the cross of our Lord Jesus Christ."(Gal. 6:14 KJV).

Now the real nature of Calvinistic soteriology becomes plain. It is no artificial oddity, nor a product of over-bold logic. Its central confession, that *God saves sinners*, that *Christ redeemed us by his blood*, is the witness both of the Bible and of the believing heart. The Calvinist is the Christian who confesses before men in his theology just what he believes in his heart before God when he prays. He thinks and speaks at all times of the sovereign grace of God in the way that every Christian does when he pleads for the souls of others, or when he obeys the impulse of worship that rises unbidden within him, prompting him to deny himself all praise and to give all the glory of his salvation to his Savior.

Calvinism is the natural theology written on the heart of the new man in Christ, whereas Arminianism is an intellectual sin of infirmity, natural only in the sense in which all such sins are natural, even to the regenerate. Calvinistic thinking is the Christian being himself on the intellectual level; Arminian thinking is the Christian failing to be himself through the weakness of the flesh. Calvinism is what the Christian church has always held and taught when its mind has not been distracted by controversy and false traditions from attending to what Scripture actually says; that is the significance of the

Patristic testimonies to the teaching of the "five points," which can be quoted in abundance. (Owen appends a few on redemption; a much larger collection may be seen in John Gill's *The Cause of God and Truth*.) So that really it is most misleading to call this soteriology "Calvinism" at all, for it is not a peculiarity of John Calvin and the divines of Dort, but a part of the revealed truth of God and the catholic Christian faith. "Calvinism" is one of the "odious names" by which down the centuries prejudice has been raised against it. But the thing itself is just the biblical gospel.[5]

Owen's Objective

In the light of these facts, we can now give a direct answer to the questions with which we began.

"Surely all that Owen is doing is defending limited atonement?" Not really. He is doing much more than that. Strictly speaking, the aim of Owen's book is not defensive at all, but constructive. It is a biblical and theological enquiry; its purpose is simply to make clear what Scripture actually teaches about the central subject of the gospel—the achievement of the Savior. As its title proclaims, it is "a treatise of the redemption and reconciliation that is in the blood of Christ: with the merit thereof, and the satisfaction wrought thereby." The question that Owen, like the Dort divines before him, is really concerned to answer is just this: what is the gospel? All agree that it is a proclamation of Christ as Redeemer, but there is a dispute as to the nature and extent of his redeeming work. Well, what saith the

---

5. C. H. Spurgeon was thus abundantly right when he declared:

> I have my own private opinion that there is no such thing as preaching Christ and Him crucified, unless we preach what is nowadays called Calvinism. It is a nickname to call it Calvinism; Calvinism is the gospel, and nothing else. I do not believe we can preach the gospel . . . unless we preach the sovereignty of God in His dispensation of grace; nor unless we exalt the electing, unchangeable, eternal, immutable, conquering love of Jehovah; nor do I think we can preach the gospel unless we base it upon the special and particular redemption of His elect and chosen people which Christ wrought out upon the Cross; nor can I comprehend a gospel which lets saints fall away after they are called.

C. H. Spurgeon, *The Early Years, Autobiography*, vol. 1 (London: Banner of Truth, 1962), 172.

Scripture? What aim and accomplishment does the Bible assign to the work of Christ? This is what Owen is concerned to elucidate.

It is true that he tackles the subject in a directly controversial way and shapes his book as a polemic against the "spreading persuasion . . . of a *general ransom*, to be paid by Christ for all; that he dies to redeem *all and every one*."[6] But his work is a systematic expository treatise, not a mere episodic wrangle. Owen treats the controversy as providing the occasion for a full display of the relevant biblical teaching in its own proper order and connection. As in Hooker's *Laws of Ecclesiastical Polity*, the polemics themselves are incidental and of secondary interest; their chief value lies in the way that the author uses them to further his own design and carry forward his own argument.

That argument is essentially very simple. Owen sees that the question that has occasioned his writing—the extent of the atonement—involves the further question of its nature, since if it was offered to save some who will finally perish, then it cannot have been a transaction securing the actual salvation of all for whom it was designed. But, says Owen, this is precisely the kind of transaction that the Bible says it was. The first two books of his treatise are a massive demonstration of the fact that according to Scripture the Redeemer's death actually saves his people, as it was meant to do. The third book consists of a series of sixteen arguments against the hypothesis of universal redemption, all aimed to show, on the one hand, that Scripture speaks of Christ's redeeming work as effective, which precludes its having been intended for any who perish, and, on the other, that if its intended extent had been universal, then *either* all will be saved (which Scripture denies, and the advocates of the "general ransom" do not affirm), *or else* the Father and the Son have failed to do what they set out to do—"which to assert," says Owen, "seems to us blasphemously injurious to the wisdom, power and perfection of God, as likewise derogatory to the worth

6. John Owen, *Works*, 10:159.

and value of the death of Christ." Owen's arguments ring a series of changes on this dilemma.[7]

Finally, in the fourth book, Owen shows with great cogency that the three classes of texts alleged to prove that Christ died for persons who will not be saved (those saying that he died for "the world," for "all," and those thought to envisage the perishing of those for whom he died), cannot on sound principles of exegesis be held to teach any such thing; and, further, that the theological inferences by which universal redemption is supposed to be established are really quite fallacious. The true evangelical evaluation of the claim that Christ died for every man, even those who perish, comes through at point after point in Owen's book. So far from magnifying the love and grace of God, this claim dishonors both it and him, for it reduces God's love to an impotent wish and turns the whole economy of "saving" grace, so-called ("saving" is really a misnomer on this view), into a monumental divine failure. Also, so far from magnifying the merit and worth of Christ's death, it cheapens it, for it makes Christ die in vain. Lastly, so far from affording faith additional encouragement, it destroys the scriptural ground of assurance altogether, for it denies that the knowledge that Christ died for me (or did or does anything else for me) is a sufficient ground for inferring my eternal salvation; my salvation, on this view, depends not on what Christ did for me, but on what I subsequently do for myself.

Thus this view takes from God's love and Christ's redemption the glory that Scripture gives them and introduces the anti-scriptural principle of self-salvation at the point where the Bible explicitly says: "not of works, lest any man should boast" (Eph. 2:9 KJV). You cannot have it both ways: an atonement of universal extent is a depreciated atonement. It has lost its saving power; it leaves us to save ourselves. The doctrine of the general ransom must accordingly be rejected, as Owen rejects it, as a grievous mistake. By contrast, however, the doctrine that Owen sets out, as he himself shows, is both biblical and God-honoring. It exalts Christ, for it teaches Christians to glory in his cross alone and to draw their hope and

7. Ibid.

assurance only from the death and intercession of their Savior. It is, in other words, genuinely evangelical. It is, indeed, the gospel of God and the catholic faith.

It is safe to say that no comparable exposition of the work of redemption as planned and executed by the triune Jehovah has ever been done since Owen published his. None has been needed. Discussing this work, Andrew Thomson notes how Owen "makes you feel when he has reached the end of his subject, that he has also exhausted it."[8] That is demonstrably the case here. His interpretation of the texts on the point of issue is sure; his power of theological construction is superb; nothing that needs discussing is omitted, and (so far as this writer can discover) no arguments for or against his position have been used since his day that he has not himself noted and dealt with. One searches his book in vain for the leaps and flights of logic by which Reformed theologians are supposed to establish their positions; all that one finds is solid, painstaking exegesis and a careful following through of biblical ways of thinking. Owen's work is a constructive, broad-based biblical analysis of the heart of the gospel and must be taken seriously as such. It may not be written off as a piece of special pleading for a traditional shibboleth, for nobody has a right to dismiss the doctrine of the limitedness, or particularity, of atonement as a monstrosity of Calvinistic logic until he has refuted Owen's proof that it is part of the uniform biblical presentation of redemption, clearly taught in plain text after plain text. And nobody has done that yet.

Understanding the Gospel Biblically

"You talked about recovering the gospel," said our questioner; "don't you mean that you just want us all to become Calvinists?"

This question presumably concerns not the word but the thing. Whether we call ourselves Calvinists hardly matters; what matters is that we should understand the gospel biblically. But that, we think, does in fact mean understanding it as historic Calvinism does. The alternative is to misunderstand and distort it. We said earlier that

8. "Life of John Owen," in John Owen, *Works*, 1:38.

modern evangelicalism, by and large, has ceased to preach the gospel in the old way, and we frankly admit that the new gospel, insofar as it deviates from the old, seems to us a distortion of the biblical message. And we can now see what has gone wrong. Our theological currency has been debased. Our minds have been conditioned to think of the cross as a redemption that does less than redeem, and of Christ as a Savior who does less than save, and of God's love as a weak affection that cannot keep anyone from hell without help, and of faith as the human help that God needs for this purpose.

As a result, we are no longer free either to believe the biblical gospel or to preach it. We cannot believe it, because our thoughts are caught in the toils of synergism. We are haunted by the Arminian idea that if faith and unbelief are to be responsible acts, they must be independent acts; hence we are not free to believe that we are saved entirely by divine grace through a faith that is itself God's gift and flows to us from Calvary. Instead, we involve ourselves in a bewildering kind of double-think about salvation, telling ourselves one moment that it all depends on God and next moment that it all depends on us. The resultant mental muddle deprives God of much of the glory that we should give him as author and finisher of salvation, and ourselves of much of the comfort we might draw from knowing that God is for us.

And when we come to preach the gospel, our false preconceptions make us say just the opposite of what we intend. We want (rightly) to proclaim Christ as Savior, yet we end up saying that Christ, having made salvation possible, has left us to become our own saviors. It comes about in this way. We want to magnify the saving grace of God and the saving power of Christ. So we declare that God's redeeming love extends to everyone, and that Christ has died to save every man, and we proclaim that the glory of divine mercy is to be measured by these facts. And then, in order to avoid universalism, we have to depreciate all that we were previously extolling, and to explain that, after all, nothing that God and Christ have done can save us unless we add something to it; the decisive factor that actually saves us is our own believing.

What we say comes to this—that Christ saves us with our help; and what that means, when one thinks it out, is this—that we save ourselves with Christ's help. This is a hollow anticlimax. But if we start by affirming that God has a saving love for all, and Christ died a saving death for all, and yet balk at becoming universalists, there is nothing else that we can say. And let us be clear on what we have done when we have put the matter in this fashion. We have not exalted grace and the cross; we have cheapened them. We have limited the atonement far more drastically than Calvinism does, for whereas Calvinism asserts that Christ's death, as such, saves all whom it was meant to save, we have denied that Christ's death, as such, is sufficient to save any of them.[9] We have flattered impenitent sinners by assuring them that it is in their power to repent and believe, though God cannot make them do it. Perhaps we have also trivialized faith and repentance in order to make this assurance plausible ("it's very simple—just open your heart to the Lord . . ."). Certainly, we have effectively denied God's sovereignty and undermined the basic conviction of true religion—that man is always in God's hands. In truth, we have lost a great deal. And it is, perhaps, no wonder that our preaching begets so little reverence and humility, and that our professed converts are so self-confident and so deficient in self-knowledge, and in the good works that Scripture regards as the fruit of true repentance.

9. Compare this from C. H. Spurgeon:

> We are often told that we limit the atonement of Christ, because we say that Christ has not made a satisfaction for all men, or all men would be saved. Now, our reply to this is, that, on the other hand, our opponents limit it: we do not. The Arminians say, Christ died for all men. Ask them what they mean by it. Did Christ die so as to secure the salvation of all men? They say, "No, certainly not." We ask them the next question—Did Christ die so as to secure the salvation of any man in particular? They answer "No." They are obliged to admit this, if they are consistent. They say, "No. Christ has died that any man may be saved if"—and then follow certain conditions of salvation. Now, who is it that limits the death of Christ? Why, you. You say that Christ did not die so as infallibly to secure the salvation of anybody. We beg your pardon, when you say we limit Christ's death; we say, "No, my dear sir, it is you that do it." We say Christ so died that he infallibly secured the salvation of a multitude that no man can number, who through Christ's death not only may be saved, but are saved, must be saved and cannot by any possibility run the hazard of being anything but saved. You are welcome to your atonement; you may keep it. We will never renounce ours for the sake of it.

It is from degenerate faith and preaching of this kind that Owen's book could set us free. If we listen to him, he will teach us both how to believe the Scripture gospel and how to preach it. For the first: he will lead us to bow down before a sovereign Savior who really saves, and to praise him for a redeeming death that made it certain that all for whom he died will come to glory. It cannot be overemphasized that we have not seen the full meaning of the cross till we have seen it as the divines of Dort display it—as the center of the gospel, flanked on the one hand by total inability and unconditional election, and on the other by irresistible grace and final preservation—for the full meaning of the cross only appears when the atonement is defined in terms of these four truths. Christ died to save a certain company of helpless sinners upon whom God had set his free saving love. Christ's death ensured the calling and keeping—the present and final salvation—of all whose sins he bore. That is what Calvary meant, and means. The cross *saved*; the cross *saves*. This is the heart of true evangelical faith; as Cowper sang:

> Dear dying Lamb, Thy precious blood
> Shall never lose its power,
> Till all the ransomed church of God
> Be saved to sin no more.

This is the triumphant conviction that underlay the old gospel, as it does the whole New Testament. And this is what Owen will teach us unequivocally to believe.

Then, second, Owen could set us free, if we would hear him, to preach the biblical gospel. This assertion may sound paradoxical, for it is often imagined that those who will not preach that Christ died to save every man are left with no gospel at all. On the contrary, however, what they are left with is just the gospel of the New Testament. What does it mean to preach "the gospel of the grace of God"? Owen only touches on this briefly and incidentally,[10] but his comments are full of light. Preaching the gospel, he tells

10. See John Owen, *Works*, 10:311–16, 404–10.

us, is not a matter of telling the congregation that God has set his love on each of them and Christ has died to save each of them, for these assertions, biblically understood, would imply that they will all infallibly be saved, and this cannot be known to be true. The knowledge of being the object of God's eternal love and Christ's redeeming death belongs to the individual's assurance,[11] which in the nature of the case cannot precede faith's saving exercise; it is to be inferred from the fact that one has believed, not proposed as a reason why one should believe. According to Scripture, preaching the gospel is entirely a matter of proclaiming to men, as truth from God which all are bound to believe and act on, the following four facts:

1) that all men are sinners and cannot do anything to save themselves;

2) that Jesus Christ, God's Son, is a perfect Savior for sinners, even the worst;

3) that the Father and the Son have promised that all who know themselves to be sinners and put faith in Christ as Savior shall be received into favor, and none cast out—which promise is "a certain infallible truth, grounded upon the superabundant sufficiency of the oblation of Christ in itself, for whomsoever [fewer or more] it be intended";[12]

4) that God has made repentance and faith a duty, requiring of every man who hears the gospel "a serious full recumbency and rolling of the soul upon Christ in the promise of the gospel, as an all-sufficient Savior, able to deliver and save to the utmost them that come to God by him; ready, able and

11. "What, I pray, is it according to Scripture, for a man to be assured that Christ died for him in particular? Is it not the very highest improvement of faith? doth it not include a sense of the spiritual love of God shed abroad in our hearts? Is it not the top of the apostle's consolation, Rom. viii. 34, and the bottom of all his joyful assurance, Gal. ii. 20?" (Ibid., 10:409).
12. Ibid., 10:315.

willing, through the preciousness of his blood and sufficiency of his ransom, to save every soul that shall freely give up themselves unto him for that end."[13]

The preacher's task, in other words, is to *display Christ*, to explain man's need of him, his sufficiency to save, and his offer of himself in the promises as Savior to all who truly turn to him; and to show as fully and plainly as he can how these truths apply to the congregation before him. It is not for him to say, nor for his hearers to ask, for whom Christ died in particular. "There is none called on by the gospel once to enquire after the purpose and intention of God concerning the particular object of the death of Christ, every one being fully assured that his death shall be profitable to them that believe in him and obey him." After saving faith has been exercised, "it lies on a believer to assure his soul, according as he find the fruit of the death of Christ in him and towards him, of the good-will and eternal love of God to him in sending his Son to die for him in particular";[14] but not before. The task to which the gospel calls him is simply to exercise faith, which he is both warranted and obliged to do by God's command and promise.

Some comments on this conception of what preaching the gospel means are in order.

First, we should observe that the old gospel of Owen contains no less full and free an offer of salvation than its modern counterpart. It presents ample grounds for faith (the sufficiency of Christ and the promise of God), and cogent motives to faith (the sinner's need and the Creator's command, which is also the Redeemer's invitation). The new gospel gains nothing here by asserting universal redemption. The old gospel, certainly, has no room for the cheap sentimentalizing that turns God's free mercy to sinners into a constitutional soft-heartedness on his part that we can take for granted; nor will it countenance the degrading presentation of Christ as the baffled Savior, balked in what he hoped to do by human unbelief; nor

13. Ibid., 10:407f.
14. Loc. cit.

will it indulge in maudlin appeals to the unconverted to let Christ save them out of pity for his disappointment. The pitiable Savior and the pathetic God of modern pulpits are unknown to the old gospel. The old gospel tells men that they need God, but not that God needs them (a modern falsehood); it does not exhort them to pity Christ but announces that Christ has pitied them, though pity was the last thing they deserved. It never loses sight of the divine majesty and sovereign power of the Christ whom it proclaims but rejects flatly all representations of him that would obscure his free omnipotence.

Does this mean, however, that the preacher of the old gospel is inhibited or confined in offering Christ to men and inviting them to receive him? Not at all. In actual fact, just because he recognizes that divine mercy is sovereign and free, he is in a position to make far more of the offer of Christ in his preaching than is the expositor of the new gospel; for this offer is itself a far more wonderful thing on his principles than it can ever be in the eyes of those who regard love to all sinners as a necessity of God's nature, and therefore a matter of course. To think that the holy Creator, who never needed man for his happiness and might justly have banished our fallen race forever without mercy, should actually have chosen to redeem some of them! And that his own Son was willing to undergo death and descend into hell to save them! And that now from his throne he should speak to ungodly men as he does in the words of the gospel, urging upon them the command to repent and believe in the form of a compassionate invitation to pity themselves and choose life! These thoughts are the focal points round which the preaching of the old gospel revolves. It is all wonderful, just because none of it can be taken for granted.

But perhaps the most wonderful thing of all—the holiest spot in all the holy ground of gospel truth—is the free invitation that "the Lord Christ" (as Owen loves to call him) issues repeatedly to guilty sinners to come to him and find rest for their souls. It is the glory of these invitations that it is an omnipotent King who gives them, just as it is a chief part of the glory of the enthroned Christ that he condescends still to utter them. And it is the glory of the gospel ministry that the preacher goes to men as Christ's ambassador, charged to deliver the King's invitation personally to every sinner present and to summon them all to turn and live. Owen himself enlarges on this in a passage addressed to the unconverted.

> Consider the infinite condescension and love of Christ, in his invitations and calls of you to come unto him for life, deliverance, mercy, grace, peace and eternal salvation. Multitudes of these invitations and calls are recorded in the Scripture, and they are all of them filled up with those blessed encouragements which divine wisdom knows to be suited unto lost, convinced sinners. . . . In the declaration and preaching of them, Jesus Christ yet stands before sinners, calling, inviting, encouraging them to come unto him.
>
> This is somewhat of the word which he now speaks unto you: Why will ye die? why will ye perish? why will ye not have compassion on your own souls? Can your hearts endure, or can your hands be strong, in the day of wrath that is approaching? . . . Look unto me, and be saved; come unto me, and I will ease you of all sins, sorrows, fears, burdens, and give rest unto your souls. Come, I entreat you; lay aside all procrastinations, all delays; put me off no more; eternity lies at the door...do not so hate me as that you will rather perish than accept of deliverance by me.
>
> These and the like things doth the Lord Christ continually declare, proclaim, plead and urge upon the souls of sinners. . . . He doth it in the preaching of the word, as if he were present with you, stood amongst you, and spake personally to every one of you. . . . He hath appointed the ministers of the gospel to appear before you, and to deal with you in his stead, avowing as his own the invitations which are given you in his name. (2 Cor. 1:19–20)[15]

These invitations are *universal*; Christ addresses them to sinners, as such, and every man, as he believes God to be true, is bound to treat them as God's words to him personally and to accept the universal assurance that accompanies them, that all who come to Christ will be received. Again, these invitations are *real*; Christ genuinely offers

15. Ibid., 1:422.

himself to all who hear the gospel and is in truth a perfect Savior to all who trust him. The question of the extent of the atonement does not arise in evangelistic preaching; the message to be delivered is simply this—that Christ Jesus, the sovereign Lord, who died for sinners, now invites sinners freely to himself. God commands all to repent and believe; Christ promises life and peace to all who do so. Furthermore, these invitations are *marvelously gracious*; men despise and reject them and are never in any case worthy of them, and yet Christ still issues them. He need not, but he does. "Come unto me . . . and I will give you rest" remains his word to the world, never cancelled, always to be preached. He whose death has ensured the salvation of all his people is to be proclaimed everywhere as a perfect Savior, and all men invited and urged to believe on him, whoever they are, whatever they have been. Upon these three insights the evangelism of the old gospel is based.

It is a very ill-informed supposition that evangelistic preaching that proceeds on these principles must be anemic and halfhearted by comparison with what Arminians can do. Those who study the printed sermons of worthy expositors of the old gospel, such as Bunyan (whose preaching Owen himself much admired), or Whitefield, or Spurgeon, will find that in fact they hold forth the Savior and summon sinners to him with a fullness, warmth, intensity, and moving force unmatched in Protestant pulpit literature. And it will be found on analysis that the very thing that gave their preaching its unique power to overwhelm their audiences with brokenhearted joy at the riches of God's grace—and still gives it that power, let it be said, even with hardboiled modern readers—was their insistence on the fact that grace is *free*. They knew that the dimensions of divine love are not half understood till one realizes that God need not have chosen to save nor given his Son to die; nor need Christ have taken upon him vicarious damnation to redeem men, nor need he invite sinners indiscriminately to himself as he does; but that all God's gracious dealings spring entirely from his own free purpose. Knowing this, they stressed it, and it is this stress that sets their evangelistic preaching in a class by itself.

Other evangelicals, possessed of a more superficial and less adequate theology of grace, have laid the main emphasis in their gospel preaching on the sinner's need of forgiveness, or peace, or power, and on the way to get them by "deciding for Christ." It is not to be denied that their preaching has done good (for God will use his truth, even when imperfectly held and mixed with error), although this type of evangelism is always open to the criticism of being too man-centered and pietistic; but it has been left (necessarily) to Calvinists and those who, like the Wesleys, fall into Calvinistic ways of thought as soon as they begin a sermon to the unconverted, to preach the gospel in a way that highlights above everything else the free love, willing condescension, patient long-suffering, and infinite kindness of the Lord Jesus Christ. And, without doubt, this is the most scriptural and edifying way to preach it; for gospel invitations to sinners never honor God and exalt Christ more, nor are more powerful to awaken and confirm faith, than when full weight is laid on the free omnipotence of the mercy from which they flow. It looks, indeed, as if the preachers of the old gospel are the only people whose position allows them to do justice to the revelation of divine goodness in the free offer of Christ to sinners.

Then, in the second place, the old gospel safeguards values that the new gospel loses. We saw before that the new gospel, by asserting universal redemption and a universal divine saving purpose, compels itself to cheapen grace and the cross by denying that the Father and the Son are sovereign in salvation; for it assures us that, after God and Christ have done all that they can, or will, it depends finally on each man's own choice whether God's purpose to save him is realized or not.

This position has two unhappy results. The first is that it compels us to misunderstand the significance of the gracious invitations of Christ in the gospel of which we have been speaking, for we now have to read them, not as expressions of the tender patience of a mighty Sovereign, but as the pathetic pleadings of impotent desire; and so the enthroned Lord is suddenly metamorphosed into a weak, futile figure tapping forlornly at the door of the human heart, which he is powerless to open. This is a shameful dishonor to the Christ of the New Testament. The second implication is equally serious, for this view in effect denies our dependence on God when it comes to vital decisions, takes us out of his hand, tells us that we are, after all, what sin taught us to think we were—masters of our fate, captains of our souls—and so undermines the very foundation of man's religious relationship with his Maker. It can hardly be wondered at that the converts of the new gospel are so often both irreverent and irreligious, for such is the natural tendency of this teaching.

The old gospel, however, speaks very differently and has a very different tendency. On the one hand, in expounding man's need of Christ, it stresses something that the new gospel effectively ignores— that sinners cannot obey the gospel, any more than the law, without renewal of heart. On the other hand, in declaring Christ's power to save, it proclaims him as the Author and Chief Agent of conversion, coming by his Spirit as the gospel goes forth to renew men's hearts and draw them to himself. Accordingly, in applying the message, the old gospel, while stressing that faith is man's duty, stresses also that faith is not in man's power, but that God must give what he commands. It announces not merely that men *must* come to Christ for salvation, but also that they *cannot* come unless Christ himself draws them. Thus it labors to overthrow self-confidence, to convince sinners that their salvation is altogether out of their hands, and to shut them up to a self-despairing dependence on the glorious grace of a sovereign Savior, not only for their righteousness but for their faith too.

It is not likely, therefore, that a preacher of the old gospel will be happy to express the application of it in the form of a demand to "decide for Christ," as the current phrase is. For, on the one hand, this phrase carries the wrong associations. It suggests voting a person into office—an act in which the candidate plays no part beyond offering himself for election, and everything then being settled by the voter's independent choice. But we do not vote God's Son into office as our Savior, nor does he remain passive while preachers campaign on his behalf, whipping up support for his cause. We ought not to think of evangelism as a kind of electioneering. And then, on the other hand, this phrase obscures the very thing that is essential in repentance and faith—the denying of self in a personal approach to Christ. It is not at all obvious that deciding *for* Christ is the same as coming *to* him and resting *on* him and turning *from* sin and self-effort; it sounds like something much less, and is accordingly calculated to instill defective notions of what the gospel really requires of sinners. It is not a very apt phrase from any point of view.

To the question, what must I do to be saved? the old gospel replies: believe on the Lord Jesus Christ. To the further question, what does it mean to believe on the Lord Jesus Christ? its reply is: it means knowing oneself to be a sinner, and Christ to have died for sinners; abandoning all self-righteousness and self-confidence, and casting oneself wholly upon him for pardon and peace; and exchanging one's natural enmity and rebellion against God for a spirit of grateful submission to the will of Christ through the renewing of one's heart by the Holy Ghost. And to the further question still, how am I to go about believing on Christ and repenting if I have no natural ability to do these things? it answers: look to Christ, speak to Christ, cry to Christ, just as you are; confess your sin, your impenitence, your unbelief, and cast yourself on his mercy; ask him to give you a new heart, working in you true repentance and firm faith; ask him to take away your evil heart of unbelief and to write his law within you, that you may never henceforth stray from him. Turn to him and trust him as best you can and pray for grace to turn and trust more thoroughly; use the means of grace expectantly, looking to Christ to draw near to you as you seek to draw near to him; watch, pray, and read and hear God's Word, worship and commune with God's people, and so continue till you know in yourself beyond doubt that you are indeed a changed being, a penitent believer, and the new heart that you desired has been put within you. The emphasis in this advice is on the need to call upon Christ directly, as the very first step.

> Let not conscience make you linger,
> Nor of fitness fondly dream;
> All the fitness He requireth
> Is to feel your need of Him—

So do not postpone action till you think you are better, but honestly confess your badness and give yourself up here and now to the Christ who alone can make you better; and wait on him till his light rises in your soul, as Scripture promises that it shall do. Anything less than this direct dealing with Christ is disobeying the gospel. Such is the exercise of spirit to which the old evangel summons its hearers. "I believe—help thou mine unbelief": this must become their cry.

And the old gospel is proclaimed in the sure confidence that the Christ of whom it testifies, the Christ who is the real speaker when the scriptural invitations to trust him are expounded and applied, is not passively waiting for man's decision as the word goes forth, but is omnipotently active, working with and through the word to bring his people to faith in himself. The preaching of the new gospel is often described as the task of "bringing men to Christ" as if only men move while Christ stands still. But the task of preaching the old gospel could more properly be described as bringing Christ to men, for those who preach it know that as they do their work of setting Christ before men's eyes, the mighty Savior whom they proclaim is busy doing his work through their words, visiting sinners with salvation, awakening them to faith, drawing them in mercy to himself.

It is this older gospel that Owen will teach us to preach: the gospel of the sovereign grace of God in Christ as the Author and Finisher of faith and salvation. It is the only gospel that can be preached on Owen's principles, but those who have tasted its sweetness will not in any case be found looking for another. In the matter of believing and preaching the gospel, as in other things, Jeremiah's words still have their application: "Thus saith the Lord, Stand ye in the ways, and see, and ask for the old paths, where is the good way, and walk therein, and ye shall find rest for your souls" (Jer. 6:16 KJV). To find ourselves debarred, as Owen would debar us, from taking up with the fashionable modern substitute gospel may not, after all, be a bad thing, either for us or for the church.

More might be said, but to go further would be to exceed the limits of an introductory essay. The foregoing remarks are made simply to show how important it is at the present time that we should attend most carefully to Owen's analysis of what the Bible says about the saving work of Christ.

Owen's Treatise

It only remains to add a few remarks about this treatise itself. It was Owen's second major work, and his first masterpiece. (Its predecessor, *A Display of Arminianism*, published in 1642, when Owen was twenty-six, was a competent piece of prentice-work, rather of the nature of a research thesis.)

The Death of Death is a solid book, made up of detailed exposition and close argument, and requires hard study, as Owen fully realized; a cursory glance will not yield much. ("Reader . . . if thou are, as many in this pretending age, *a sign or title gazer*, and comest into books as Cato into the theatre, to go out again—thou has had thy entertainment; farewell!"[16]) Owen felt, however, that he had a right to ask for hard study, for his book was a product of hard work ("a more than seven-years' serious inquiry . . . into the mind of God about these things, with a serious perusal of all which I could attain that the wit of man, in former or latter days, hath published in opposition to the truth"[17]), and he was sure in his own mind that a certain finality attached to what he had written. ("Altogether hopeless of success I am not; but fully resolved

16. Opening words, "To the Reader," John Owen, *Works*, 10:149.
17. Loc. cit.

that I shall not live to see a solid answer given unto it."[18]) Time has justified his optimism.[19]

Something should be said about his opponents. He is writing against three variations on the theme of universal redemption: that of classical Arminianism, noted earlier; that of the theological faculty at Saumur (the position known as Amyraldism, after its leading exponent); and that of Thomas More, a lay theologian of East Anglia. The second of these views originated with a Scots professor at Saumur, John Cameron; it was taken up and developed by two of his pupils, Amyraut (Amyraldus) and Testard, and became the occasion of a prolonged controversy in which Amyraut, Daillé, and Blondel were opposed by Rivet, Spanheim, and Des Marets (Maresius). The Saumur position won some support among Reformed divines in Britain, being held in modified form by (among others) Bishops Ussher and Davenant, and Richard Baxter. None of these, however, had advocated it in print at the time when Owen wrote.[20]

Goold's summary of the Saumur position may be quoted:

Admitting that, by the purpose of God, and through the death of Christ, the elect are infallibly secured in the enjoyment of salvation,

18. Ibid., 10:156.

19. Owen indicates more than once that for a complete statement of the case against universal redemption he would need to write a further book, dealing with "the other part of this controversy, concerning the cause of sending Christ" (pp. 245, 295). Its main thesis, apparently, would have been that "the fountain and cause of God's sending Christ, is his eternal love to his elect, and to them alone" (p. 131), and it would have contained "a more large explication of God's purpose of election and reprobation, showing how the death of Christ was a means set apart and appointed for the saving of his elect, and not at all undergone or suffered for those which, in his eternal counsel, he did determine should perish for their sins" (p. 245). It looks, therefore, as if it would have included the "clearing of our doctrine of reprobation, and of the administration of God's providence towards the reprobates, and over all their actions," which Owen promised in the epistle prefixed to A Display of Arminianism (Works, 10:9), but never wrote. However, we can understand his concluding that it was really needless to slaughter the same adversary twice.

20. Davenant's Duae Dissertationes, one of which defends universal redemption on Amyraldean lines, came out posthumously in 1650. Owen was not impressed and wrote of it: "I undertake to demonstrate that the main foundation of his whole dissertation about the death of Christ, with many inferences from thence, are neither formed in, nor founded on the word; but that the several parts therein are mutually conflicting and destructive of each other" (Works, 10:433; 1650). Baxter wrote a formal disputation defending universal redemption but never printed it; it was published after his death, however, in 1694.

they contended for an antecedent decree, by which God is free to give salvation to all men through Christ, on the *condition* that they believe on him. Hence their system was termed *hypothetic(al) universalism*. The vital difference between it and the strict Arminian theory lies in the absolute security asserted in the former for the spiritual recovery of the elect. They agree, however, in attributing some kind of universality to the atonement, and in maintaining that, on a certain *condition*, within the reach of fulfilment by all men . . . all men have access to the benefits of Christ's death.

From this, Goold continues:

The readers of Owen will understand . . . why he dwells with peculiar keenness and reiteration of statement upon a refutation of the conditional system. . . . It was plausible; it had many learned men for its advocates; it had obtained currency in the foreign churches; and it seems to have been embraced by More.[21]

More is described by Thomas Edwards as "a great Sectary, that did much hurt in Lincolnshire, Norfolk, and Cambridgeshire; who was famous also in Boston, [King's] Lynn, and even in Holland, and was followed from place to place by many."[22] Baxter's description is kinder: "a Weaver of *Wisbitch* and *Lyn*, of excellent Parts."[23] (More's doctrine of redemption, of course, was substantially Baxter's own.) Owen, however, has a poor view of his abilities and makes no secret of the fact.

More's book, *The Universality of God's Free Grace in Christ to Mankind*, appeared in 1646 (not, as Goold says, 1643) and must have exercised a considerable influence, for within three years it had evoked four weighty works that were in whole or part polemics against it: *A Refutation . . . of Thomas More*, by Thomas Whitfield, 1646; *Vindiciae Redemptionis*, by John Stalham, 1647; *The Universalist Examined and Convicted*, by Obadiah Howe, 1648; and Owen's own book, published in the same year.

21. "Prefatory Note," in *Works*, 10:140.
22. *Gangraena* (1646), 2:86.
23. Richard Baxter, *Reliquiae Baxterianae*, i:50.

More's exposition seems to be of little intrinsic importance; Owen, however, selects it as the fullest statement of the case for universal redemption that had yet appeared in English and uses it unmercifully as a chopping-block. The modern reader, however, will probably find it convenient to skip the sections devoted to refuting More (I:viii., the closing pages of I:iii. and IV:vi.) on his first passage through Owen's treatise.

Finally, a word about the style of this work. There is no denying that Owen is heavy and hard to read. This is not so much due to obscure arrangement as to two other factors. The first is his lumbering literary gait. "Owen travels through it [his subject] with the elephant's grace and solid step, if sometimes also with his ungainly motion." says Thomson.[24] That puts it kindly. Much of Owen's prose reads like a roughly-dashed-off translation of a piece of thinking done in Ciceronian Latin. It has, no doubt, a certain clumsy dignity; so has Stonehenge; but it is trying to the reader to have to go over sentences two or three times to see their meaning, and this necessity makes it much harder to follow an argument. The present writer, however, has found that the hard places in Owen usually come out as soon as one reads them aloud.

The second obscuring factor is Owen's austerity as an expositor. He has a lordly disdain for broad introductions that ease the mind gently into a subject and for comprehensive summaries that gather up scattered points into a small space. He obviously carries the whole of his design in his head and expects his readers to do the same. Nor are his chapter divisions reliable pointers to the structure of his discourse, for though a change of subject is usually marked by a chapter division, Owen often starts a new chapter where there is no break in the thought at all. Nor is he concerned about literary proportions; the space given to a topic is determined by its intrinsic complexity rather than its relative importance, and the reader is left to work out what is basic and what is secondary by noting how things link together. Anyone who seriously tackles *The Death of Death* will probably find it helpful to use a pencil

24. "Life of John Owen," *Works.*

and paper in his study of the book and jot down the progress of the exposition.

We would conclude by repeating that the reward to be reaped from studying Owen is worth all the labor involved and by making the following observations for the student's guidance. (1) It is important to start with the epistle "To the Reader," for there Owen indicates in short compass what he is trying to do and why. (2) It is important to read the treatise as a whole, in the order in which it stands, and not to jump into Parts III and IV before mastering the contents of Parts I and II, where the biblical foundations of Owen's whole position are laid. (3) It is hardly possible to grasp the strength and cogency of this massive statement on a first reading. The work must be read and reread to be appreciated.

Epilogue

Christ-Centered Means Cross-Centered

J. I. Packer and Mark Dever

J. I. Packer remembers:

Some sixty years ago, Dr. D. Martyn Lloyd-Jones addressed a pre-term conference of the Oxford Inter-Collegiate Christian Union (OICCU), Oxford's Inter-Varsity chapter, of which I was a member. I had not heard him speak before, but he had the reputation of being Britain's supreme gospel preacher, and I listened to him with intense interest. He dug into the first two chapters of 1 Corinthians, which he described as perhaps the two most important chapters of the Bible for mid-twentieth-century Christians. I well recall how he began his message on Christ crucified according to 1:17–31. He told us that the hymn he had had us sing to start the session was the only one he could find in our hymn book that focused directly on the meaning of the cross in and of itself, as distinct from the blessings that flow to us from it and the grateful adoration it evokes. He said that this reflected the modern weakness of celebrating benefits from the cross

without seeking clarity as to what Christ's dying had done to achieve
them for us.

The hymn in question was the following, written by Fanny
Crosby (Mrs. A. R. Cousin). Physically almost blind from bad
surgery in childhood, she saw and stated the biblical significance
of the cross with great precision. I had never met the hymn before,
and I have never forgotten it since; it anchors my heart and fuels
my praying still.

> O Christ, what burdens bowed thy head!
>   Our load was laid on thee;
> Thou stoodest in the sinner's stead,
>   Didst bear all ill for me.
> A victim led, thy blood was shed,
>   Now there's no load for me.
>
> Death and the curse were in our cup:
>   O Christ, 'twas full for thee!
> But thou hast drained the last dark drop,
>   'Tis empty now for me;
> That bitter cup, love drank it up,
>   Thy bruising healeth me.
>
> Jehovah lifted up his rod;
>   O Christ, it fell on thee!
> Thou wast sore stricken of thy God;
>   There's not one stroke for me.
> Thy tears, thy blood, beneath it flowed;
>   Thy bruising healeth me.
>
> For me, Lord Jesus, thou hast died,
>   And I have died in thee;
> Thou'rt risen—my bands are all untied,
>   And now thou liv'st in me;
> When purified, made white and tried,
>   Thy glory then for me!

Along with that hymn, I have since come to treasure this one, by the more rhapsodic Charles Wesley, which covers similar ground from a similar standpoint and with a similar thrust.

> All ye that pass by
> To Jesus draw nigh;
> To you is it nothing that Jesus should die?
> Our ransom and peace,
> Our surety he is,
> Come, see if there ever was sorrow like his.

> The Lord in the day
> Of his anger did lay
> Our sins on the Lamb, and he bore them away;
> He died to atone
> For sins not his own,
> The Father hath punished for us his dear Son.

> Love moved him to die,
> On this I rely;
> My Savior hath loved me, I cannot tell why;
> But this I can tell,
> He loved me so well
> As to lay down his life to redeem me from hell.

> With joy we approve
> The plan of his love;
> A wonder to all, both below and above!
> When time is no more
> We still shall adore
> That ocean of love, without bottom or shore!

To anyone who is flagging in prayer and fellowship with God, I would recommend meditation on such words as these. A renewed sighting of the cross will always invigorate and motivate. Let me quote another of my favorite hymns on that.

> We sing the praise of him who died,
> Of him who died on the cross;

The sinner's hope let men deride,
    For this we count the world but loss.

Inscribed upon the cross we see
    In shining letters, "God is love";
He bears our sins upon the tree,
    He brings us mercy from above.

The cross! It takes our guilt away,
    It holds the fainting spirit up;
It cheers with hope the gloomy day,
    And sweetens every bitter cup.

It makes the coward spirit brave,
    And nerves the feeble arm for fight;
It takes its terror from the grave
    And gilds the bed of death with light.

The balm of life, the cure of woe,
    The measure and the pledge of love;
The sinner's refuge here below,
    The angels' theme in heaven above.

I do not see how Christian devotion can sustain itself if we lose sight of the cross—that is, the cross-work, as we may call it—of our Lord Jesus Christ.

The Centrality of Christ

The cross of Christ, thus understood, is, as the preceding chapters have argued, the heart of the apostles' gospel and of their piety and praise as well; so surely it ought to be central in our own proclamation, catechesis, and devotional practice. True Christ-centeredness is, and ever must be, cross-centeredness. The cross on which the divine-human mediator hung, and from which he rose to reign on the basis and in the power of his atoning death, must become the vantage point from which we survey the whole of human history and human life, the reference point for explaining all that has gone wrong in the world everywhere and all that God has done and will do to put it right, and the center point for fixing the flow of doxology and devotion from our hearts. Healthy, virile, competent Christianity depends on clear-headedness about the cross; otherwise we are always off-key. And clear-headedness about the cross, banishing blurriness of mind, is only attained by facing up to the reality of Christ's blood-sacrifice of himself in penal substitution for those whom the Father had given him to redeem.

Why then is it that in today's churches, even in some professedly evangelical congregations, this emphasis is rare? Why is it that in seminary classrooms, professional theological guilds, Bible teaching conferences, and regular Sunday preaching, not to mention the devotional books that we write for each other, so little comparatively is said about the heart-stirring, life-transforming reality of penal substitution? Several reasons spring to mind.

First, we forget that the necessity of retribution for sin is an integral expression of the holiness of God, and we sentimentalize his love by thinking and speaking of it without relating it to this necessity. This leaves us with a Christ who certainly embodies divine wisdom and goodwill, who certainly has blazed a trail for us through death into life, and who through the Spirit certainly stands by each of us as friend and helper (all true, so far as it goes), but who is not, strictly speaking, a *redeemer* and an *atoning sacrifice* for us at all.

Second, in this age that studies human behavior and psychology with such sustained intensity, knowledge of our sins and sinfulness as seen by God has faded, being overlaid by techniques and routines for self-improvement in terms of society's current ideals of decency and worthwhileness of life. It is all very secular, even when sponsored by churches, as it often is, and it keeps us from awareness of our own deep guilty and shameful alienation from God, which only the Savior, who in his sinlessness literally bore the penalty of our sins in our place, can deal with.

Third, in an age in which historic Christianity in the West is under heavy pressure and is marginalized in our post-Christian communities, we are preoccupied with apologetic battles, doctrinal and ethical, all along the interface of Christian faith and secularity—battles in which we are for the most part forced to play black, responding to the opening gambits of our secular critics. Constant concern to fight and win these battles diverts our attention from thorough study of the central realities of our own faith, of which the atonement is one.

Fourth, heavyweight scholars in our own ranks, as we have seen, line up from time to time with liberal theologians to offer revisionist, under-exegeted accounts of Bible teaching on the atonement, accounts which in the name of Scripture (!) play down or reject entirely the reality of penal substitution as we have been expounding it. The effect is that whereas from the sixteenth to the nineteenth century evangelicals stood solid for penal substitution against unitarianism (Socinianism) and deism, and taught this truth as no less central to the gospel than the incarnation itself, today it is often seen as a disputed and disputable option that we can get on quite well without, as many already are apparently doing.

What in the way of understanding our Savior and our salvation we lose, however, if we slip away from penal substitution, is, we think, incalculable.

The Centrality of the Cross

Early in the visionary chapters of the book of Revelation, where images are prodigally piled up, one on another, in order to convey thoughts to readers' minds, the Lord Jesus is announced as "the Lion of the tribe of Judah" who will open the scroll for the consummation of world history (5:5). But the Lion appears not as a lion but as "a Lamb standing, as though it had been slain" (v. 6 ESV). The Lamb appears thereafter twenty-eight more times, battling, conquering, shepherding, and finally functioning as the lamp that gives permanent light to his bride, the holy city, new Jerusalem, that is, the church perfected in glory (21:23, cf. 22:1–5). In this book, then, the slain Lamb is a key image for the Lord Jesus Christ. Where did it come from? Clearly, from (1) the Passover lamb, the blood of which shielded Israel from the destroyer at the time of

150

the Exodus, plus (2) the God-prescribed ritual of killing a lamb, with the transgressor's hand on its head, as a sin offering (Lev. 4:32–35), plus (3) the required daily sacrifice of two lambs as sinful Israel's offering to its holy god (Ex. 29:38–42; Num. 28:3–6), plus (4) Isaiah's description of God's servant, the vicarious sufferer who became a sin offering, as being led "like a lamb . . . to the slaughter" (Isa. 53:7), plus (5) John the Baptist's identification of Jesus as "the Lamb of God, who takes away the sin of the world" (John 1:29, 36). And for the Lamb to be the lamp of the city of God means that the thought of the Son of God made flesh and slaughtered for our sins in order to save us will never leave the minds of glorified saints as they fellowship with the Father and the Son and will frame all their thinking about everything else.

So all we who hope for the life of heaven ourselves, and especially those among us who as pastors are statedly committed to prepare others for that heavenly life, will do well to adjust our thinking here and now to the absolute and abiding centrality of the atoning cross in Christian life here and hereafter and to labor to express this awareness in all our preaching, teaching, and modeling of Christianity, day by day.

Books on the Cross of Christ

Ligon Duncan

These lists and the following select, annotated bibliography are intended for Christians who, having been edified by the wonderful pieces by J. I. Packer and Mark Dever in this little book, are thirsting for more good material that will aid them in deepening their understanding of the meaning and significance and consequences of the death of our Savior, Jesus Christ. I hope that these reading suggestions will be helpful to many, not only in providing them with a "must read" list on the atonement, but also in providing them recommendations for other church leaders and members.

If you have no idea where to start, look at the following lists of suggestions. If you don't know anything about the books in the various lists provided, take a look at the annotations to the full alphabetical bibliography following. In those annotations I hope to provide enticing and summarizing comments that will help draw you to books that will be helpful to your soul and ministry.

Ten on the Atonement

Am I loopy enough to attempt to suggest a top-ten list of "must reads" on the atonement? Apparently so. The motivation is simple though: the annotated bibliography that follows may seem overwhelming to some, so this shorter "best-of" list may help. This list of ten books leans to the popular and devotional side, but all the entries are sound and substantial. I've tried here to put them in a good order for reading.

1. Piper, John. *Fifty Reasons Why Jesus Came to Die*. Wheaton, IL: Crossway Books, 2006.
2. Mahaney, C. J. *Living the Cross Centered Life*. Sisters, OR: Multnomah, 2006.
3. Leahy, Frederick S. *The Cross He Bore, The Victory of the Lamb*, and *Is It Nothing to You?* Edinburgh: Banner of Truth, 1996, 2001, and 2004.
4. Ryken, Philip Graham, and James Montgomery Boice. *The Heart of the Cross*. Wheaton, IL: Crossway Books, 2005.
5. Warfield, Benjamin B. *The Saviour of the World*. Edinburgh: Banner of Truth, 1991.
6. Morris, Leon. *The Atonement: Its Meaning and Significance*. Leicester: Inter-Varsity, 1983.
7. Murray, John. *Redemption Accomplished and Applied*. Grand Rapids, MI: Eerdmans, 1955.
8. Stott, John R. W. *The Cross of Christ*. Leicester: Inter-Varsity, 1986.
9. Jeffery, Steve, Michael Ovey, and Andrew Sach. *Pierced for our Transgressions*. Wheaton, IL: Crossway Books, 2007.
10. Calvin, John. *Institutes of the Christian Religion*, 2 vols. Translated by F. L. Battles. Philadelphia: Westminster, 1960 (see esp. 1:464–534).

Short, Popular Introductions

If you are looking for a good launching point into the vast ocean of sound teaching available on the doctrine of the atonement, and you'd like to read something accessible that will give you a feel for the subject and be edifying at the same time, try the following. To find out more about them, read the annotated bibliography at the end of this section. I'm tempted to suggest that you read them in this order: Piper, then Shaw/Edwards, then Wells, then Bridges/Bevington, and finally, Morris.

- Bridges, Jerry, and Bob Bevington. *The Great Exchange*. Wheaton, IL: Crossway Books, 2007. Jerry Bridges loves George Smeaton on the atonement, important work that this book popularizes.

- Morris, Leon. *The Atonement: Its Meaning and Significance*. Leicester: Inter-Varsity, 1983. Though more challenging than the other four books on this list, this is a worthy shorter volume.

- Piper, John. *Fifty Reasons Why Jesus Came to Die*. Wheaton, IL: Crossway Books, 2006. Designed for evangelistic use, this book can be read in little chunks. Chock full of devotional worth.

- Shaw, Ian J., and Brian H. Edwards. *The Divine Substitute: The Atonement in the Bible and History*. Leominster, UK: DayOne, 2006. In less than 150 pages Shaw and Edwards provide a sound biblical and historical introduction to the doctrine of the atonement.

- Wells, Tom. *A Price for a People: The Meaning of Christ's Death*. Edinburgh: Banner of Truth, 1992. Wells's book focuses on the biblical material. He is a Baptist pastor in Ohio.

Sermons

Make a habit of reading and listening to sermons on the atoning work of Christ. There is no better way to prepare to teach and preach and live the cross yourself. So read and listen to the masters preach the cross.

- Lloyd-Jones, D. Martyn. *Romans: Atonement and Justification*. Edinburgh: Banner of Truth, 1970. What can one say about Lloyd-Jones? John Piper listens to him! These sermons contain powerful models for preaching atonement and justification.

- Martin, Hugh. *Christ for Us*. Edinburgh: Banner of Truth, 1998. If you think Martin's *The Atonement* is truth on fire (and it is!), then buckle your seatbelts for his preaching.

- Spurgeon, Charles H. *Spurgeon's Sermons on the Cross of Christ*. Grand Rapids, MI: Kregel, 1993. The prince of preachers. Read anything and everything you can get by him, and make a beeline for the cross.

- Warfield, Benjamin B. *The Saviour of the World*. Edinburgh: Banner of Truth, 1991. You'll never be able to think about John 3:16 in the same way again after reading Warfield's sermon.

Pastoral Application of the Doctrine of the Atonement

Do you need help in seeing how the cross applies to life and ministry? Here are two good examples:

- Carson, D. A. *The Cross and Christian Ministry*. Grand Rapids, MI: Baker Books, 2004. Carson shows us how the cross works out (or should work out) in the church's gospel ministry.

- Mahaney, C. J. *Living the Cross Centered Life*. Sisters, OR: Multnomah, 2006. Do you want the atonement worked into your bones? Read this.

Systematic Theologies

If you want to dip into some representative systematic theologies, but you don't know where to start, here are five good entries with strengths all their own.

- Berkhof, Louis. *Systematic Theology*. New Combined Edition. Grand Rapids, MI: Eerdmans, 2006. Berkhof is hard to beat for historical overview, clear orthodox presentation, and discerning evaluation (see esp. 367–99).

- Boyce, James P. *Abstract of Systematic Theology*. Hanford, CA: den Dulk Foundation. A classic, solid, Baptist presentation on the atonement (see esp. 295–340).

- Calvin, John. *Institutes of the Christian Religion*. 2 vols. Translated by F. L. Battles. Philadelphia: Westminster, 1960. The fountainhead of the Reformed tradition. Do not miss Calvin on this topic!

- Grudem, Wayne. *Systematic Theology*. Grand Rapids, MI: Zondervan, 1994. Probably the easiest to read of these five books. Great for use as a teaching outline on the subject (see esp. 568–607).

- Reymond, Robert L. *A New Systematic Theology of the Christian Faith*. Nashville: Thomas Nelson, 1998. An extensive exegetical-theological treatment by a solid, conservative, contemporary theologian (see esp. 623–795).

Chronological Listing of Works of Historic Significance on the Atonement

Two criteria have ruled above others in the making of this brief list: significance and edification. One could have made a very long list that stretches back in time (I can hear some asking, "Where are Irenaeus, Origen, Augustine, Anselm, and Luther?"), or that ranges a bit more broadly in more recent literature (one could ask, "Where are Albrecht Ritschl, McLeod Campbell, F. D. Maurice, P. T. Forsyth, Gustaf Aulén, James Denney, Emil Brunner, and Karl Barth?"). But this list is deliberately restrictive. The works included are significant in themselves and in their contexts and are of the highest value for the positive edification of the reader. Again, see the annotated bibliography at the end for descriptions of these authors and books.

1559: Calvin, John. *Institutes of the Christian Religion.* 2 vols. Translated by F. L. Battles. Philadelphia: Westminster, 1960. Most important theological work of the last half millennium.

1647: Owen, John. *The Death of Death in the Death of Christ.* Edinburgh: Banner of Truth, 1959. The classic work by the greatest of the British Calvinists.

1679: Turretin, Francis. *Institutes of Elenctic Theology.* 3 vols. Edited by James T. Dennison. Translated by George M. Griger. Phillipsburg, NJ: P&R, 1994. The "queen of the sciences," according to the "king" of seventeenth-century Protestant Orthodoxy (see esp. 2:375–499).

1861: Heppe, Heinrich. *Reformed Dogmatics.* Translated by G. T. Thomson. Grand Rapids, MI: Baker Books, 1978. Quotations from the main continental Reformed scholars during the age of Protestant Orthodoxy (see esp. 448–509).

1867: Hodge, A. A. *The Atonement.* Memphis, TN: Footstool, 1987. The classic nineteenth-century Princeton treatment of this subject.

1868: Smeaton, George. *Christ's Doctrine of the Atonement.* Edinburgh: Banner of Truth, 1991. One of the Free Church of Scotland's brightest lights expounds and defends the doctrine.

1870: ———. *The Doctrine of the Atonement according to the Apostles.* Peabody, MA: Hendrickson, 1988. The sequel to *Christ's Doctrine of the Atonement* by one of the leading Scottish pastor-theologians of his day.

1870: Martin, Hugh. *The Atonement*. Greenville, SC: Reformed Academic Press, 1997. Heat and light. Truth on fire. A combination of orthodoxy, originality, and passion.

1887: Boyce, James P. *Abstract of Systematic Theology*. Hanford, CA: den Dulk Foundation. Classic nineteenth-century treatment. Clear and sound; really helpful for outlining the subject.

1895–1901: Bavinck, Herman. *Reformed Dogmatics*, 4 vols. Edited by John Bolt. Translated by John Vriend. Grand Rapids, MI: Baker Academic, 2003–2008. Major early-twentieth-century orthodox Dutch work, now fully available in English (see esp. 3:323–482).

1902–1917: Warfield, Benjamin B. *The Person and Work of Christ*. Phillipsburg, NJ: Presbyterian and Reformed, 1950. Greatest of the Princeton theologians. Reading this makes you mad that Warfield didn't write a systematic theology.

1939: Berkhof, Louis. *Systematic Theology*. New Combined Edition. Grand Rapids, MI: Eerdmans, 2006. The standard English-language Reformed systematic theology. The starting point for all reading in systematics for English readers.

1955: Murray, John. *Redemption Accomplished and Applied*. Grand Rapids, MI: Eerdmans, 1955. This is, simply put, a "must read." If you haven't read it, you are not ready to talk theology.

1965: Morris, Leon. *The Apostolic Preaching of the Cross.* Leicester: Inter-Varsity, 1965. The classic, modern, evangelical exposition and defense of the historic Christian doctrine.

1986: Stott, John R. W. *The Cross of Christ.* Leicester: Inter-Varsity, 1986. Stott's *magnum opus.* Essential reading.

2007: Jeffery, Steve, Michael Ovey, and Andrew Sach. *Pierced for Our Transgressions.* Nottingham, UK: Inter-Varsity; Wheaton, IL: Crossway Books, 2007. The latest major evangelical entry into the fray with those denying penal substitution. Excellent.

Important Confessional Statements on the Atonement

Don't cheat yourself by failing to read what the evangelical churches have confessed about the meaning and accomplishment of the death of Christ over the last five hundred years. As important as are the theological works I've just listed, Protestants have always given even more weight to what the churches have corporately confessed as their public theology, that is, what the churches have professed to be the teaching of Scripture and their public embrace of it. You can read these short confessional statements in a matter of minutes, but spend the rest of your life understanding them more deeply and appreciating their beautiful and faithful testimony to biblical truth.

1530: *Augsburg Confession* (Lutheran), 3. http://www.ctsfw.edu/etext/boc/ac/augustana03.asc.

1536: *Smalcald Articles* (Lutheran), pt. 1; pt. 2, 1–5: "Office and Work of Christ, or Our Redemption." http://www.lcms.org/graphics/assets/media/LCMS/smalcald.pdf.

1560: *Scots Confession* (Presbyterian), 9.
http://www.creeds.net/reformed/Scots/ scots.
htm#Passion.

1561: *Belgic Confession* (Reformed), 21.
http://www.carm.org/creeds/ belgic.
htm#Article%2021.

1563: *Thirty-Nine Articles* (Anglican), 2 and 11.
http://www.acl.asn.au/the-thirty-ninearticles.

1562–1564: *Second Helvetic Confession* (Reformed), 11.
http://www.sacred-texts.com/chr/ 2helvcnf.htm.

1618–1619: *Canons of Dordt* (Reformed) Head 2.
http://www.mb-soft.com/believe/txh/ dort1.htm.

1647: *Westminster Confession* (Presbyterian, Anglican,
Congregationalist), 8.3–8.
http://www.reformed.org/documents/wcf_with_
proofs.

1658: *Savoy Declaration* (Congregationalist), 8.3–8.
http://www.creeds.net/congregational/savoy/index.
htm.

1689: *London Confession* (Baptist), 8.3–10.
http://www.vor.org/truth/1689/1689bc08.html.

1833: *New Hampshire Confession* (Baptist), 4.
http://www.spurgeon.org/~phil/creeds/nh_conf.
htm#4

1858: *Abstract of Principles* (Southern Baptist), 7.
http://www.founders.org/abstract.html.

Annotated Bibliography

Ligon Duncan

Bavinck, Herman. *Reformed Dogmatics*, 4 vols. Edited by John Bolt. Translated by John Vriend. Grand Rapids, MI: Baker Academic, 2003–2008.

> Bavinck (1854–1921) was a giant of the late nineteenth- and early twentieth-century Protestant theological world. His complete massive systematic theology is finally now available in an English translation. The third volume contains his treatment of the work of Christ. Bavinck groups his presentation of this material under the headings of "Christ's Humiliation" and "Christ's Exaltation"—a classic way of approaching this subject in dogmatics.

Berkhof, Louis. *Systematic Theology*. New Combined Edition. Grand Rapids, MI: Eerdmans, 2006.

> This volume by Berkhof (1873–1954) has probably been the most widely used modern Reformed systematic theology text in English since the middle of the twentieth century. It is an important reference work for the shelf of every Protestant pastor. I highly recommend the most recent edition by Eerdmans (they are calling it the "New Combined Edition") with a new preface by Richard Muller, which includes Berkhof's "Intro-

duction to the Study of Systematic Theology." Berkhof is brilliant at giving good, clear, quick summaries of the history of a doctrine and various schools of thought, and he is superb at outlining the main points of discussion in relation to any given doctrine. His treatment of the doctrine of the atonement is solid and helpful.

Boyce, James P. *Abstract of Systematic Theology.* Hanford, CA: den Dulk Foundation.

Boyce (1827–1888) was the founder of the Southern Baptist Theological Seminary (SBTS), and really "the leading founder of the vision for organized theological education within the Southern Baptist Convention," and a man of powerful intellect, great learning, and cultural breadth. He was the son of one of the wealthiest men in South Carolina, and grew up in one of the most cultured cities in America of his day, Charleston, South Carolina. He was educated in some of the best institutions of that time (Charleston College, Brown University, and Princeton Seminary), sat under the preaching of outstanding ministers in his youth (Basil Manly Sr., Richard Fuller, and James Henley Thornwell) and studied with the principal conservative American theologians of his era (including Archibald Alexander and Charles Hodge). This volume contains his class notes from SBTS. It gives insight into the mainstream Baptist theology of the atonement in the nineteenth century and provides a useful outline for study.

Bridges, Jerry, and Bob Bevington. *The Great Exchange.* Wheaton, IL: Crossway Books, 2007.

Jerry Bridges (1929–) is one of the very best and most reliable popularizers of sound Bible teaching today. This book is subtitled, "My Sin for His Righteousness—An Exposition of the Atonement of Jesus Christ, Patterned after the Apostles' Doctrine of the Atonement by George Smeaton." Smeaton's book is one of Jerry Bridges's all-time favorites, and, so, in this more easily readable rendition of Smeaton, Bridges and Bevington give the reader a feast for the soul. If you want to put a book into the hands of layfolk that covers the ground that Smeaton covers (see the entries on Smeaton in this annotated bibliography), but is more accessible, this is it. In terms of applying the cross and the gospel to daily life, no one does a better job than Bridges. Another helpful book by Jerry Bridges is *The Gospel for Real Life* (Colorado Springs: NavPress, 2002).

Calvin, John. *Institutes of the Christian Religion.* 2 vols. Translated by F. L. Battles. Philadelphia: Westminster, 1960.

Calvin (1509–1564) is generally regarded as one of the best exegetes and theologians in the whole history of Christian theology. Usually ranked with Augustine and Aquinas in stature and influence, Calvin is one of the principle fountainheads of the now half-millennium-old Reformed tradition. The *Institutes* is his *magnum opus.* I commend to you the Battles edition rather than the older Beveridge translation. Calvin's treatment of the atonement comes in Book 2 of the *Institutes* under the heading "The Knowledge of God the Redeemer in Christ, Disclosed to the Fathers under the Law, and then to us in the Gospel." Beginning with chapter 12 and running through chapter 17 especially, Calvin's treatment of the person and work of Christ will well repay your study. To be noted is Calvin's deliberate and emphatic retention of the category of "merit" in relation to the work of Christ. He says: "There are certain perversely subtle men who—even though they confess that we receive salvation through Christ—cannot bear to hear the word 'merit,' for they think that it obscures God's grace." In contrast, Calvin asserts that the Bible teaches that "by his obedience, Christ truly acquired and merited grace for us with his Father."

Carson, D. A. *The Cross and Christian Ministry.* Grand Rapids, MI: Baker Books, 2004.

D. A. Carson (1946–) is yet another important evangelical figure. Long considered in the very first rank of international evangelical scholarship, Carson was born in Canada (thus his fluent French), studied chemistry and mathematics at McGill University in Montreal, and then graduated from Central Baptist Seminary in Toronto; thereafter he pastored Richmond Baptist Church in British Columbia. He did his PhD at Cambridge under the renowned scholar Barnabas Lindars and then taught at Northwest Baptist Theological College in Vancouver, serving as founding dean of its seminary. Ken Kantzer, the dean of Trinity Evangelical Divinity School in Deerfield, Illinois, coaxed him there to teach in 1978, where he remains to this day, now as research professor of New Testament. Carson has held editorial posts with the *Trinity Journal* (editor, 1980–1986) and the *Journal of the Evangelical Theological Society* (book review editor, 1979–1986). He is editor of the New Studies in Biblical Theology series (Intervarsity/Apollos), as well as editor of the Pillar Commentary series (InterVarsity/Apollos/Eerdmans), just to name a few. *The Cross and Christian Ministry* focuses on 1 Corinthians, and by careful exegesis Carson draws applications from the work of Christ on the cross for the church's manner of ministry. Carson, along with Tim Keller, gives leadership to the Gospel Coalition (see www.thegospelcoalition.org).

Denney, James. *The Death of Christ*. London: Hodder and Stoughton, 1902.

Denney's work is a classic and reflects its author's intense evangelistic passion. Denney (1856–1917) was a Scottish Presbyterian minister and professor in the Free Church and then in the United Free Church of Scotland. He was brilliant—earning a rare "double first" in classics and philosophy from Glasgow University—and pious—reading Spurgeon's sermons helped him retain evangelical and Reformed convictions while many of his most admired contemporaries and teachers were falling under the influence of liberal theology. He is famous for his statement: "I haven't the faintest interest in any theology which doesn't help me to evangelize." Though Denney held views that made evangelicals on both sides of the Atlantic somewhat uneasy, his book is in the main a robust defense of classic penal substitutionary atonement, though he did not use legal, judicial, or forensic terms in relation to the atonement. Denney also rejects the category of "merit" in relation to the work of Christ, as well as any doctrine of mystical union with Christ. He allowed for only a consequent moral union.

Forsyth, Peter T. *The Cruciality of the Cross*. Eugene, OR: Wipf and Stock, 1997.

Forsyth (1842–1921) was a Scottish Congregational pastor and theologian who studied at Göttingen under Albrecht Ritschl. Though Forsyth was early influenced by higher critical approaches to Christianity, he increasingly rejected and polemicized against liberal theology. A central issue of conflict and resolution in his own theological journey was the doctrine of the atoning work of Christ. This book (first published by Hodder and Stoughton, London, 1910) is one of his best-known and helpful expositions of this theme. Forsyth, under the lingering influence of Adolf von Harnack, unfortunately held on to a kenotic doctrine of the incarnation, although he had a twist on his view, different from the well-known version of Bishop Charles Gore. His rebuke of liberal Christianity is set out in what may be his most famous work, *The Person and Place of Christ* (1909). Forsyth is considered—accurately or not—a sort of proto-neo-orthodox theologian.

Grudem, Wayne. *Systematic Theology*. Grand Rapids, MI: Zondervan, 1994.

Wayne Grudem (1948–) is a well-known evangelical scholar who, along with John Piper, has done as much as anyone to foster a wider understanding and embrace of the Bible's teaching on male-female role relationships in the home and church—a view known as "complementarianism"—in the context of our dominant egalitarian culture. Grudem is also an accomplished teacher of biblical doctrine. His *Systematic Theology* has a very helpful section on the atonement—he argues for "definite atonement" or "particular redemption" but proposes some cautions—with a good bibliography of works by Anglican, Arminian, Baptist, Dispensational, Lutheran, Reformed, Charismatic, and Roman Catholic systematic treatments of the doctrine of the atonement. Grudem's work may be the most concise and accessible, comprehensive, one-volume systematic theology on the market today. Though it is not a factor in this discussion, the reader may want to note that Grudem is a non-cessationist, or continuationist, on the issue of New Testament spiritual gifts.

Helm, Paul. *Calvin and the Calvinists*. Edinburgh: Banner of Truth, 1982.

Since at least the time of Perry Miller and Karl Barth, a myth has been popular in some circles of historical theological studies that there is a major divide between Calvin and the so-called Protestant Scholastic theologians of the seventeenth century. Consequently, if you are reading this material, you'll find Calvin contrasted with Owen, or pitted against the Westminster Confession or the Puritans. The shorthand description of this historiography is "Calvin versus the Calvinists," and no one has done more to explode this myth than Richard Muller (read *Christ and the Decree*). Paul Helm (1940–, brilliant, English, Baptist professor of philosophy) responds in this little book to a "Calvin versus the Calvinists" dissertation by R. T. Kendall called "Calvin and English Calvinism to 1649." Helm focuses on the question of the atonement. The book gives you a good, short, historical, and theological introduction to the subject matter. Helm is right. By the way, Banner of Truth publishes many excellent works (www.banneroftruth.org).

Hengel, Martin. *Crucifixion in the Ancient World and the Folly of the Message of the Cross*. Philadelphia: Fortress Press, 1977.

This volume contains tremendous background information on the act of crucifixion. One reviewer says of it: "In a comprehensive and detailed survey on its remarkably widespread employment in the Roman empire, Dr. Hengel (1926–) examines the way in which 'the most vile death of the cross' was regarded in the Greek-speaking world and particularly in Roman-occupied Palestine. His conclusions bring out more starkly than ever the offensiveness of the Christian message: Jesus not only died an unspeakably cruel death, he underwent the most contemptible abasement that could be imagined. So repugnant was the gruesome reality that a natural tendency prevails to blunt, remove, or domesticate its scandalous impact. Yet any discussion of a 'theology of the cross' must be preceded by adequate comprehension of both the nature and extent of this scandal." Hengel taught New Testament and Early Judaism at Tübingen.

Heppe, Heinrich. *Reformed Dogmatics*. Translated by G. T. Thomson. Grand Rapids, MI: Baker Books, 1978.

This book, first published in German in 1861 (translated and published in English in 1950, and then reprinted by Baker Books in the U.S. in 1978), is an important source book of quotations in the main topical headings of systematic theology drawn from the writings of some of the most important Protestant Scholastic—better, "Protestant Orthodox"—theologians of the seventeenth century. It will give you a quick feel for the language and categories they employed and will supply you with great quotes to use for teaching. Karl Barth himself was deeply respectful of this volume, even though his own theology departed from it. Indeed, Barth paid these theologians a great compliment when he said of them, in contrast to the theologians of his day and many of our own, "You always know what they are saying." Heppe (1820–1879) himself was, to borrow the words of Lowell Zuck, "a Melanchthonian Liberal in the nineteenth-century German Reformed Church," but the theologians and quotations he assembled in this important collection are thoroughly evangelical and orthodox. This book may be hard to find, but it is well worth finding, obtaining, having, and reading. It has been recently reprinted by the Wakeman Trust in England. I keep hearing that Richard Muller is working on producing a more accurate, expanded, and retranslated edition.

Hill, Charles H., and Frank A. James, eds. *The Glory of the Atonement*. Downers Grove, IL: InterVarsity, 2004.

This is a solid collection of exegetical, historical, and practical essays on the atonement by well-known evangelical scholars, among them D. A. Carson, Richard Gaffin, Henri Blocher, Sinclair Ferguson, J. I. Packer, Kevin Vanhoozer, Joel Beeke, and more, produced as a *festschrift* for the important, modern, French, evangelical and Reformed, Baptist theologian, Roger Nicole—himself one of the leading historians and theologians of our era regarding the doctrine of the atonement. The volume offers a scholarly overview of the Old and New Testaments' teaching on the atonement and provides a scholarly historical treatment of the doctrine of atonement in the theology of select key figures in Christian history. It concludes with two excellent pieces focused on applying the doctrine of the atonement, one by J. I. Packer on atonement and the Christian life and the other by Sinclair Ferguson on preaching the atonement. Nicole himself provides a little gem at the end of the book in his "Postscript on Penal Substitution." Charles Hill (1956–) is a world-class New Testament and patristic scholar, and Frank James (1953–) is a recognized Peter Martyr Vermigli expert.

Hodge, A. A. *The Atonement*. Memphis, TN: Footstool, 1987.

The son of famous Princeton theologian Charles Hodge, A. A. Hodge (1823–1886) succeeded his father as professor of systematic theology at Princeton. Known for his powerful, reverent, and acute mind, A. A. Hodge along with B. B. Warfield played an important role in defending the historic, Christian, high view of Scripture (inerrancy). He wrote this little treatise on the atonement in 1867. If you can find it, in any edition or printing, get it. It offers an excellent presentation of the nature and application of the atonement of Christ.

Jeffery, Steve, Michael Ovey, and Andrew Sach. *Pierced for Our Transgressions*. Nottingham, UK: Inter-Varsity; Wheaton, IL: Crossway Books, 2007.

Aptly subtitled *Recovering the Glory of Penal Substitution*, this important book is a team effort at expounding, commending, and defending the historic, evangelical, biblical doctrine of the atonement—a view very much under assault from a variety of directions in modern day evangelicalism. If you have been shaken by these recent attacks on penal substitution, you need to read this book. The utterly impressive list of endorsers of the volume tells you (1) how important this doctrine is; (2) how neglected, misunderstood, unknown, underappreciated, and unpreached it is; (3) how endangered it is; and (4) how good a job this book does of defending it. Anglican Bishop N. T. Wright thought this volume important enough to issue a scathing review of it. In their completely courteous but devastating rejoinder to Bishop Wright, Jeffery (1975–), Ovey (1958–), and Sach (1975–) showed themselves every bit a match to his prodigious scholarship, and superior in their grasp and presentation of this vital doctrine. Go to http://piercedforourtransgressions. com and read the exchange and find more resources on this vital doctrine. Jeffery and Sach are Anglican clergymen, and

Ovey is principal and lecturer in doctrine and apologetics at Oak Hill Theological College in England.

Leahy, Frederick S. *The Cross He Bore*. Edinburgh: Banner of Truth, 1996.

———. *Is It Nothing to You?* Edinburgh: Banner of Truth, 2004.

———. *The Victory of the Lamb*. Edinburgh: Banner of Truth, 2001.

Leahy (1922–2006) was a revered minister in the Reformed Presbyterian Church (Northern Ireland). He served in the chair of systematic theology, apologetics, and Christian ethics in the Reformed Theological College, Belfast, and also as college principal from 1993–2002. A much-appreciated writer, his trilogy on Christ's atoning work is not to be missed.

Letham, Robert. *The Work of Christ*. Downers Grove, IL: Inter-Varsity, 1993.

Robert Letham (1947–) teaches at Wales Evangelical School of Theology and is a visiting professor of theology at Reformed Theological Seminary, Washington, DC, and adjunct professor of systematic theology at Westminster Theological Seminary, Philadelphia. Before going to Wales he was senior minister of Emmanuel Presbyterian Church (OPC), Wilmington, Delaware, and before that senior lecturer in Christian doctrine at London Bible College. He is author of a number of significant works including *The Holy Trinity* (P&R, 2004) and *Through Western Eyes* (Mentor, 2007). This solid treatment of the work of Christ is organized around what theologians call *munus triplex*, the threefold office of Christ as prophet, priest, and king. The volume shows insights from significant interactions with the Scottish Barthian school of theology and contains an appendix that recasts the traditional debates on the *extent* of the atonement by refocusing on the question of the *intent* of the atonement.

Lloyd-Jones, D. Martyn. *Romans: Atonement and Justification.* Edinburgh: Banner of Truth, 1970.

Lloyd-Jones (1899–1981), a, perhaps *the*, major British evangelical leader of the twentieth century, was one of the great preachers of his day, and a key contributor to the present resurgence of Reformed theology in the English-speaking world. J. I. Packer calls him "the greatest man I have ever known." His influence on men who themselves would become major evangelical figures was immense. "The Doctor" was a past master of doctrinal, applicatory, experiential, expository preaching. Read more about him at Dr. Martyn Lloyd-Jones Online (www.misterrichardson.com) or listen to his sermons at MLJ Recordings Trust (www.mlj.org.uk). Read Iain Murray's two-volume biography of Lloyd-Jones: *David Martyn Lloyd-Jones: The First Forty Years 1899–1939* (Banner of Truth, 1982) and *David Martyn Lloyd-Jones: The Fight of Faith 1939–1981* (Banner of Truth, 1990). The sermons in *Romans: Atonement and Justification* are from a series he preached in March 1968. This volume covers Romans 3:20–4:25 and contains riveting messages such as "Propitiation," "The Blood of Jesus Christ," and "The Vindication of God."

Macleod, Donald. *The Humiliated and Exalted Lord.* Greenville, SC: Reformed Academic Press, 1994.

Donald Macleod (1940–), principal and professor of theology at the Free Church of Scotland College, Edinburgh, is, perhaps, Scotland's best-kept secret in the late twentieth/early twenty-first century. No one preaches the cross better than Macleod. This little book is based on lectures originally given at a Theological Studies Fellowship conference in Swanwick, Derbyshire, England, in the mid-1970s. They were transcribed and published with minor editing (under the title, *Philippians 2 and Christology*) by the Universities and Colleges Christian Fellowship's (UCCF, formerly Inter-Varsity Fellowship or IVF) Theological Studies Fellowship (TSF). Macleod's chapter entitled "Love Divine, All Loves Excelling" in his book *Behold Your God* (Christian Focus Publications, 1995) contains a compelling exposition and defense of the historic Reformed doctrine of the unique love of God for the elect. Very significant in setting forth the doctrine of the nature, effect, and extent of the atonement. Visit christianfocus.com and reformedacademicpress.com.

Mahaney, C. J. *Living the Cross Centered Life*. Sisters, OR: Multnomah, 2006.

C. J. Mahaney (1953–) C. J. summarizes the gospel like this: "God sent his Son to the cross to bear his wrath for sinners like you and me." That all-important message is the core of *Living the Cross Centered Life*, subtitled *Keeping the Gospel the Main Thing*. This book weaves together content from C. J.'s two previous books, *The Cross Centered Life* and *Christ Our Mediator*. The revision retains all the wisdom of both previous books while adding even more material, showing how to center every day on the life-giving reality of the gospel. C. J. Mahaney leads Sovereign Grace Ministries (www.sovereigngraceministries.org), having pastored Covenant Life Church (www.covlife.org) in Gaithersburg, Maryland for twenty-seven years. C. J. also serves as the vice-chairman of the Council on Biblical Manhood and Womanhood (cbmw.org) and on the Council of the Alliance of Confessing Evangelicals (alliancenet. org and reformation21.org).

Martin, Hugh. *The Atonement*. Greenville, SC: Reformed Academic Press, 1997.

This work is yet another classic. Hugh Martin (1822–1885) was a minister in the Free Church of Scotland, pastoring in Panbride and Edinburgh. He was editor of the famed *The British and Foreign Evangelical Review* and *The Watchword*. Martin was not alone amongst Scottish defenders of the atonement (Robert Candlish, George Smeaton, and Thomas Crawford come readily to mind), but, according to one source, his work was "unsurpassed as a synthesis of orthodoxy and originality." This important work relates the biblical doctrine of the atonement to the covenant of grace, federal theology, and Christ's priestly office, including Christ's work of intercession, and implicitly responds to various contemporary (nineteenth-century) errors on the subject. Find it at reformedacademicpress.com.

————. *Christ for Us*. Edinburgh: Banner of Truth, 1998.

This collection of sermons displays Martin at his best, preaching the cross. Principal John Macleod of the Free College says this of him: "Dr. Martin was, in respect of sheer intellectual and spiritual power, in the very first rank of the Scottish Reformed Church during all the course of its history." Another book that displays his preaching of the cross is still in print as well, *The Shadow of Calvary* (Banner of Truth). It would be a good habit for every evangelical preacher always to be reading something on the atonement, and especially the best sermons on the atonement. Such a practice gets our hearts ready to run to the cross in our own preaching.

McDonald, H. D. *The Atonement of the Death of Christ*. Grand Rapids, MI: Baker Books, 1985.

This is an excellent reference work. It gives a helpful doctrinal, biblical, and especially historical overview of the doctrine of the atonement. McDonald (c.1910–2001) lectured for many years at London Bible College and served as vice principal. The evaluations of various historic views of the atonement are even-handed and sympathetic, but discerning.

175

Morris, Leon. *The Apostolic Preaching of the Cross*. Leicester: Inter-Varsity, 1965.

Leon Morris (1914–2006) was one of the leading evangelical New Testament scholars of the twentieth century, and served as principal of Ridley College in Melbourne, Australia. This work, rightly deemed a modern-day evangelical classic, delves into the biblical doctrine of atonement by looking at the terms and ideas of redemption, covenant, blood, Lamb of God, propitiation, reconciliation, and justification. The content is evangelical and scholarly. Written against the backdrop of, for instance, C. H. Dodd's denial of the concept of *propitiation* in favor of the idea of *expiation* (because of his rejection of the idea of the personal wrath of God, which Dodd called "a thoroughly archaic idea"), and informed by a massive, decade-long investigation not only of the biblical data, but also of its contemporary context, Morris's work established the scriptural basis of the historic, confessional, orthodox approach to the preaching of the cross. He called it not a "full-scale study of the atonement, but a necessary preliminary." Get the third revised edition. If you just can't get enough of Morris, read his massive *The Cross in the New Testament* (Grand Rapids, MI: Eerdmans, 1965).

———. *The Atonement: Its Meaning and Significance*. Leicester: Inter-Varsity, 1983.

Think of this book as a popularized version of *The Apostolic Preaching of the Cross*. From the very beginning of his academic career, Morris made the doctrine of the atonement a special point of study. It shows.

Murray, John. *Redemption Accomplished and Applied*. Grand Rapids, MI: Eerdmans, 1955.

John Murray (1898–1975) was professor of systematic theology at Westminster Theological Seminary in Philadelphia. An outstanding theologian and exegete (if you don't have his commentary on *Romans* [Eerdmans], you should), Murray penned this short but heavy classic based on a series of Sunday school lessons. Fred Zaspel says: "Every pastor should read and reread John Murray's *Redemption Accomplished and Applied* until the entire book is completely digested and has thoroughly affected his entire frame of reference. It is one of the most helpful little volumes on the work of Christ you can ever get your hands on." I agree. As I first read this book, thunder and lightning exploded all around, as my heart encountered blazing evangelical truth expressed with precision, erudition, and passion. I never fail to be moved when I return to it.

Nicole, Roger. *Standing Forth: Collected Writings of Roger Nicole.* Fearn: Mentor, 2002.

Roger Nicole (1915–) is one of the founding fathers of modern evangelicalism. He was a charter member of the Evangelical Theological Society and one of its first presidents, cofounder of the *Gordon Review* (now the *Christian Scholar's Review*), and professor at Gordon-Conwell and Reformed Seminaries for a half-century; he helped organize the *International Council on Biblical Inerrancy*, has been a contributing editor to *Christianity Today* for more than fifty years, and assisted in the production of the NIV and the *New Geneva Study Bible*. He is also an expert on the theology and history of the atonement. The center section of these collected scholarly writings of Nicole's is devoted to the atonement. In six chapters he tackles: (1) a definition of the atonement; (2) the nature of redemption; (3) Calvin's view of the extent of the atonement; (4) the controversy over universal grace in the mid-seventeenth century; (5) covenant, universal call, and definite atonement; and (6) C. H. Dodd on propitiation. Masterly.

Owen, John. *The Death of Death in the Death of Christ.* Edinburgh: Banner of Truth, 1959.

John Owen (1616–1683) was the vice chancellor of Oxford. Learn more about him at johnowen.org. Sinclair Ferguson says this about him: "To read John Owen is to enter a rare world. Whenever I return to one of his works I find myself asking 'Why do I spend time reading lesser literature?' . . . There is constantly in Owen, even when we are in the thick of him (and some of his writing is dense indeed) a doxological motive and motif. If we can persevere with his style (which becomes easier the longer we persevere), he will not fail to bring us to the feet of Jesus." J. I. Packer says, "I owe more to John Owen than to any other theologian, ancient or modern." It is not surprising then to hear theologians speak of "the three Johns" as the greatest of all Reformed thinkers: John Calvin, John Owen, and Jonathan Edwards. Owen's first published work dealt with the subject of the atonement (*A Display of Arminianism*, 1642) and the whole of volume 10 of his collected works is devoted to this topic (*The Works of John Owen, vol. 10: The Death of Christ*, Banner of Truth). *The Death of Death in the Death of Christ* (online at ccel. org/ccel/owen/deathofdeath.html, but buy the book anyway) is John Owen's definitive work on the extent of the atonement. It is a polemical work, engaging the ideas of universal redemption in Arminianism and Amyraldianism.

Peterson, David, ed. *Where Wrath and Mercy Meet*. Carlisle: Paternoster, 2001.

This is a scholarly collection of essays defending the doctrine of penal substitutionary atonement in the face of current challenges. Peterson (1944–), well known for his book *Engaging with God*, was until recently the principal of Oak Hill College (an evangelical theology faculty in England that prepares students for Anglican ministry, though it also trains students from other denominations). One of the contributors to this volume, Michael Ovey, is also one of the authors of *Pierced for Our Transgressions* and is now principal at Oak Hill College.

Where Wrath and Mercy Meet concludes with a good piece on justification by faith by the well-regarded former vice principal of Oak Hill, the prolific Alan Stibbs.

Peterson, Robert A. *Calvin and the Atonement*. Fearn: Mentor, 1999.

Robert A. Peterson (1948–) is professor of systematic theology at Covenant Theological Seminary in St. Louis, Missouri. This excellent little book first appeared with the title *Calvin's Doctrine of the Atonement* (P&R, 1983). The book is the first and only introduction to Calvin's teaching on the atonement that follows Calvin's own outline of the subject: the threefold office of Christ, and the six biblical themes of (1) Christ, the obedient second Adam; (2) Christ the Victor; (3) Christ our legal substitute; (4) Christ our sacrifice; (5) Christ our merit; and (6) Christ our example. It is commended by both J. I. Packer and Sinclair Ferguson (themselves recognized Calvin scholars), and is now in a revised edition from Christian Focus Publications under their Mentor imprint, published in 1999. I used this book to help outline my original lectures on the atonement for my systematic theology classes at Reformed Theological Seminary. Very helpful. Shows the importance of the category of merit in Calvin's theology of the atonement and beautifully sets it in the context of Calvin's devastating rejoinder to the Socinian rejection of the same.

Piper, John. *Fifty Reasons Why Jesus Came to Die*. Wheaton, IL: Crossway Books, 2006.

John Piper (1946–), along with R. C. Sproul and John MacArthur, may be the most well-known current advocate, both nationally and internationally, for the doctrines of grace. If you want to know more about his ministry visit his church web site (www.hopeingod.org) or the Desiring God web site listed below. This book was originally published in 2004 under the title *The Passion of Jesus Christ*, to take advantage of the evangelistic opportunity presented by the release of Mel Gibson's movie *The Passion of the Christ* (2004). It was rereleased with the new title in 2006. Piper grabs your attention in the book's opening lines: "The most important question of the twenty-first century is: Why did Jesus Christ come and die? To see this importance we must look beyond human causes. The ultimate answer to the question, who killed Jesus? is: God did. It is a staggering thought. Jesus was his Son! But the whole message of the Bible leads to this conclusion." To get the book, or learn more about it, visit Desiring God (www.desiringgod.org) or Crossway Books (www.crossway.org). You can browse the full text online at Crossway. Piper then proceeds to present an answer to the question, what did God achieve for sinners like us in sending his Son to die? by giving fifty short, clear, devotional expositions of key Bible texts. Gold mine.

Reymond, Robert L. *A New Systematic Theology of the Christian Faith*. Nashville: Thomas Nelson, 1998.

Robert Reymond (1932–) taught for many years at Covenant Theological Seminary in St. Louis, and since that time at Knox Seminary in Ft. Lauderdale. I had the privilege of sitting through the whole course of his systematics lectures in St. Louis, including the outstanding material recommended here on what Reymond calls the "cross work" of Christ. Reymond is at his best defending classical Christian Christology despite his non-standard views on the *filioque* clause and *monogenes* as can be seen in his outstanding book *Jesus, Divine Messiah* (P&R, 1990). His treatment of the work of Christ is perhaps the most extensive in any recent one-volume systematic theology and is a real treasure.

Ryken, Philip Graham, and James Montgomery Boice. *The Heart of the Cross*. Wheaton, IL: Crossway Books, 2005.

Philip Ryken (1966–) and James Boice (1938–2000) provide us with a superb devotional book about the cross. Good, easy, sound, helpful, rich reading. Boice, a major figure of twentieth-century evangelicalism, was a key leader in the International Council on Biblical Inerrancy and the founder of the Alliance of Confessing Evangelicals (www.alliancenet.org), and Ryken is his successor as senior minister of Tenth Presbyterian Church in Philadelphia. Visit www.tenth.org and be sure to read Ryken's "Windows on the World," or read his blog posts at www.reformation21.org. Ryken is a prolific and respected author in his own right. Don't miss Ryken and Boice's other related collaboration, *The Doctrines of Grace*, also published by Crossway, and especially its fifth chapter on particular redemption (pp. 113–34).

Shaw, Ian J., and Brian H. Edwards. *The Divine Substitute: The Atonement in the Bible and History*. Leominster, UK: DayOne, 2006.

Shaw (1961–) and Edwards (——) give a good, quick overview of the biblical teaching in approximately forty pages and then a brief, helpful survey of the doctrine of the atonement in church history (approx. 90 pages). The latter is reflective of the work of H. D. McDonald (see the notes earlier in this bibliography under H. D. McDonald's *The Atonement of the Death of Christ*). To find this book or to get more information about DayOne, another reliable publisher to frequent, go to www.dayone.co.uk or dayonebookstore.com.

Smeaton, George. *Christ's Doctrine of the Atonement*. Edinburgh: Banner of Truth, 1991.

George Smeaton (1814–1889) was a Church of Scotland minister, then a Free Church of Scotland minister, later becoming a professor at the Free Church College in Aberdeen and then at New College, Edinburgh. The noted Reformed pastor, author, and leader W. J. Grier of Belfast rightly said of Smeaton that he "was one of the brilliant galaxy of men" in the Free Church of his time. His contemporaries concurred in this assessment, James MacGregor saying of him that he possessed "the best constituted theological intellect in Christendom." Principal John Macleod describes Smeaton as "the most eminent scholar of the set of young men who with McCheyne and the Bonars sat at the feet of Chalmers." This is the first of a twin set he wrote on the doctrine of the atonement in the New Testament. It was written in the context of widespread academic defection from the historic Christian doctrine of the atonement, and is rightly judged as a classic, evangelical, orthodox exposition of this truth.

————. *The Doctrine of the Atonement according to the Apostles.* Peabody, MA: Hendrickson, 1988.

Smeaton undertook the writing of this volume upon the completion of the one just above and considered the two works as parts of a whole, intending the reader to be familiar with the principles expounded in the first volume as he or she reads the application of them in the second. Smeaton was acquainted with all the main liberal, academic treatments of the atonement of his day, in Britain and on the Continent, including Ritschl, and said of them "With all their acknowledged learning and ability, they have too much forgotten the simple function of the interpreter, and deposited their own unsatisfactory opinions or the spirit of the age in the texts which they professed to expound." A salutary and serious warning to us all.

Sproul, R. C. *The Truth of the Cross.* Orlando, FL: Reformation Trust, 2007.

R. C. Sproul (1939–) has been one of the most consistent, eloquent, popular spokesmen for resurgent Reformed theology in the last half-century in the English-speaking world. So, needless to say, we greet his book on this vital topic with anticipation. Bruce Waltke says of this new gem: *"The Truth of the Cross* is the best book on the cross I have read. It is a 'must' for every church library and a book that I will give away many times to friends. This is so because it is sober (i.e., it contains historically informed reflections on salient biblical texts), sensible (i.e., it is well-argued), simple (i.e., it holds the reader's attention through grabbing illustrations and even a seventh-grader can grasp its substance), and spiritual (i.e., it comes from a heart set ablaze by the Spirit)."

Spurgeon, Charles H. *Spurgeon's Sermons on the Cross of Christ.* Grand Rapids, MI: Kregel, 1993.

Where do you begin when it comes to the prince of preachers? Well, here's a little collection, but you need to read anything and everything you can get by Spurgeon (1834–1892). He is always and everywhere preaching the cross, but here are a few leads. Read "Particular Redemption," preached on February 28, 1858, in *Spurgeon's Sermons: Volume 4*, no. 181, and also "The Death of Christ" (January 24, 1858) in *Spurgeon's Sermons: Volume 4*, no. 173. Phil Johnson, master of all things Spurgeon, gave me a bunch of good ideas, all available via the internet (Johnson's www.spurgeon.org and http://teampyro. blogspot.com). Johnson reminded me about Tom Nettles's excellent article on Spurgeon and the atonement in the *Founder's Journal*: http://www.founders.org/FJ14/article1.html and then went on to say, "Here is a handful of Spurgeon's best sermons on the atonement, in chronological order of their publication. These are all from the New Park Street and Met Tab Pulpit series, so even though my web pages don't give full academic citations with page numbers, etc., these should be very easy to find documentation for: http://www.spurgeon. org/sermons/0007.htm, and also (same url plus) /0054.htm, /0118.htm, /0139.htm, /0141.htm, /0153.htm, /0173.htm, /0181.htm, /0228.htm, /0255.htm, /0310.htm, /0493.htm,

/1004.htm, /1910.htm, /2133.htm and /2656.htm." Get *The New Park Street Pulpit* and the *Metropolitan Tabernacle Pulpit* which continue to be available in various editions (Baker, Pilgrim, etc.).

Stott, John R.W. *The Cross of Christ*. Leicester: Inter-Varsity, 1986.

One word: classic. What can one say about dear John Stott? Alongside Carl Henry, Francis Schaeffer, Martyn Lloyd-Jones, and J. I. Packer, Stott (1921–) has been at the very center of the best of modern evangelicalism for over a half century. He was curate, then rector, and then rector emeritus of All Souls Church, Langham Place, London. He founded the Langham Partnership International and the London Institute for Contemporary Christianity. He drafted the *Lausanne Covenant*; he is a prolific author and one of the most recognized and respected leaders of world evangelicalism. Alistair McGrath calls this book, *The Cross of Christ*, Stott's "greatest and best work," and J. I. Packer says, "No other treatment of this supreme subject says so much so truly and so well." Though Stott does not address the question of the design of the extent of the atonement, and perhaps indicates that he follows in the train of J. C. Ryle as a "four-point Calvinist" Anglican who has no interest in polemicizing against five-point Calvinists, this is a kind and intelligent, but robust and rousing, defense of a real, penal, substitutionary atonement.

Tidball, Derek. *The Message of the Cross*. Downers Grove, IL: Inter-Varsity, 2001.

It required some restraint on my part not to add this to the "Short, Popular Introductions" list at the front of this bibliography. Derek Tidball (1948–) is principal of the London School of Theology, where he lectures in pastoral theology. He also served for many years as a Baptist pastor. Tidball, with Alec Motyer and John Stott, is one of the editors for InterVarsity's *Bible Speaks Today* (*BST*) series—really good Old and New Testament expositional commentaries, along with some select topical studies. He is responsible for the *BST* Bible Themes series, which has some nice entries. I love, for instance, Philip Ryken's *The Message of Salvation* in the *BST* series. *The Message of the Cross* is yet another good option to put in the hands of someone wanting to start out reading solid, accessible material on the atoning work of Christ.

Turretin, Francis. *Institutes of Elenctic Theology*. 3 vols. Edited by James T. Dennison. Translated by George M. Giger. Phillipsburg, NJ: P&R, 1994.

Turretin (1623–1687) was a towering giant of Protestant orthodoxy. It is well known that Turretin's *Institutes* (in Latin) served as the basic systematic theology textbook at Princeton Seminary during the time of Charles Hodge. The Giger translation (8,000 handwritten pages) stayed in a drawer in the seminary library for those struggling with their Latin. I myself used a typewritten version of this translation in my seminary days in the 1980s. So there was much fanfare when the whole translation finally appeared in print. Jonathan Edwards, Charles Hodge, and R. L. Dabney, to name only a few, were all dependent upon Turretin, who has been called "prince of scholastic Calvinism." Everyone from Wayne Grudem to Carl Henry to Sinclair Ferguson to Leon Morris to J. I. Packer to Roger Nicole to Richard Muller to John Frame to John Gerstner hailed the new publication of Turretin. The late James Montgomery Boice said, "If ever a great theological work has been unjustly neglected, it has been Francis Turretin's masterful volumes on the whole of Christian doctrine." Take it and read.

Warfield, Benjamin B. *The Person and Work of Christ.* Phillipsburg, NJ: Presbyterian and Reformed, 1950.

B. B. Warfield (1851–1921) "out-read, out-thought, and out-wrote every man of his generation"—so says Donald Macleod, and he's right. Time spent reading Warfield is never wasted. This volume contains some of his best work relating to the atoning work of Christ. Wayne Grudem's *Systematic Theology* (p. 605), lists some further recommended writings by Warfield on the atonement. Warfield's exegetical prowess is legendary, and it shows in his treatments here. This volume also contains the justly famous and important essay "The Emotional Life of Our Lord." Warfield is incisive and dominant in his rebuttal of error in "Modern Theories of the Atonement." Simply grasping the insights of his "New Testament Terminology of Redemption" will deliver you from all-too-common current errors. Buy the ten-volume set of *The Works of B. B. Warfield* (Baker Books) if you can get it.

————. *The Saviour of the World.* Edinburgh: Banner of Truth, 1991.

These are sermons originally preached by Warfield in the Princeton Seminary Chapel—and you'll be able to tell that by their contents—pertaining to the work of Christ. His exposition of the "all" passages and explanation of the Johannine concept of "world" are both crucial in understanding the New Testament teaching on the effect of the work of Christ. The sermon on the prodigal son needs to be read and digested by every Protestant minister in our time. It is colossally important from a gospel standpoint, because this parable is often preached in a way that truncates or warps the gospel.

Wells, Paul. *Cross Words: The Biblical Doctrine of the Atonement.* Fearn: Christian Focus Publications, 2006.

Paul Wells (1946–), originally from Liverpool, has taught theology for over thirty years at the Faculté Libre de Théologie Réformée, Aix-en-Provence, France. Iain D. Campbell, himself a superb scholar and author (read more about him at www.backfreechurch. co.uk) recently heard Paul deliver a brilliant paper at the Affinity Theology Conference (www.affinity.org.uk) on the fourth word of Jesus from the cross: "My God, My God, why have you forsaken me?" Campbell describes Paul's book this way:

Cross Words is not about the sayings of Jesus on the cross; rather it is a study on the significance of the cross-work of Jesus which uses single words as the chapter titles, words like Scandal, Lordship, Violence, Sacrifice, Penalty, and so on. The work of Jesus on the cross for our sins is central to the Christian faith. That work is what atonement is all about; and atonement, as Wells says in the opening sentence, is about right relationships. I think Paul Wells' book will become a classic too. He is writing against a background of suspicion that the older, classic works got it wrong—that we shouldn't speak of the cross as an act of Son-giving, or even of penal substitution. Some writers suggest that we need to use our imagination to find new metaphors for the cross-work of Jesus. But Wells answers these charges adequately, showing that the Bible's own 'cross-words' supply us with the only way in which we can rightly understand what Jesus did for us at Calvary. The result is a powerful book, deep yet essentially easy to read, which is extremely helpful.

Paul Wells wrote an excellent rejoinder to James Barr's really bad book *Fundamentalism.*

Wells, Tom. *A Price for a People: The Meaning of Christ's Death.* Edinburgh: Banner of Truth, 1992.

In this short, popular treatment, Wells (——) expounds the terms *redemption, reconciliation,* and *propitiation,* and then tackles the question, for whom did Christ die? *A Price for a*

People is a good place to start reading for something basic on these subjects. Wells is pastor of The King's Chapel in West Chester, Ohio (Cincinnati area), and is associated, along with Fred Zaspel, with the movement called "new covenant theology," which has no bearing on the subject matter of this book.